T0380727

WHO ARE YOU, STAKING A CLAIM IN THIS LAND?

MARJORIE K. JONES

D.D. McADORY

 www.trafford.com

North America & international
toll-free: 1 888 232 4444 (USA & Canada)
fax: 812 355 4082

WHO ARE YOU, STAKING A CLAIM IN THIS LAND?

CONTENTS

PREFACE

This book stems from life experiences in Mobile, Alabama and inspirations from my brother, Emrich C. Kenny and my best friend, Denise D. McAdory. Many of the focal points were compiled to reveal a historical gap regarding the culture of Blacks and how they lived and survived in the South during the late 40's, 50's, 60's and 70's. Based on archival research, little has been written about the following: (1) Blacks faith and religious beliefs in the 40's, 50's, 60's, and 70's in Mobile, Alabama. (2) The struggle Blacks encountered to gain economic stability and self-identity. (3) The difficulties Blacks faced in obtaining status, values, earning a living, purchasing homes and land; only to have it stolen or taken away by Whites; (4) Growing up in a predominately Black settlement called Down-The-Bay; and the devastating effects of having this neighborhood destroyed. The aforementioned are a few of the occurrences that took place during and after reconstruction in this community.

Hopefully, as a result of this endeavor others will follow our path to help regain self-identity and possession of lands taken through the judicial system during the 19th and 20th Century.

DEDICATION

THIS BOOK IS DEDICATED IN MEMORY OF LENDELL W. JONES WHO
GATHERED PICTURES AND NEWS ARTICLES WHILE EMPLOYED IN THE
POSITION OF LIBRARIAN IN THE GENEALOGY DEPARTMENT AT THE
MOBILE PUBLIC LIBRARY. OTHERS THAT INSPIRED AND SUPPORTED
THIS DISIRE TO DOCUMENT THE HISTORY OF DOWN-THE-BAY IN
MOBILE ALABAMA AND THE LOST LAND OF BLACKS ARE AS FOLLOWS:
GERTRUDE G. LEMON, GRANDMOTHER; MYRTLE B. AARON, MOTHER;
VIRGINIA ROBINSON CRAWFORD, AUNT; AND MY EXTENDED DOWN-THE-
BAY FAMILY. THESE NAMES ARE SUBMITTED ON BEHALF OF AUTHOR
MARJORIE K. JONES.

ON BEHALF OF AUTHOR DENISE D. McADORY: JOSEPH AND EPSIE
SHEPARD, GRANDPARENTS, HENRY AND ASERLENA DAVENPORTE,
PARENTS AND JOHN P. McADORY, III, SON.

A NOTE FOR READERS

It is our hope that through these historical oral experiences of the Down-The-Bay cultural life from the prospective of the authors, family elders, kin and non-kin folk that others will investigate the history of their communities. These experiences must be documented and told so that our children will have a foundation to build a family life. For Blacks the family and religious convictions is our core and, without these components, we will die and our way of life in this millennium will be a blur.

Additionally, there are several areas in the Mobile community such as: Snug Harbor, Camp Ground, Sandtown, The Bottom, Toulminville, Sand Town, Happy Hill, Black Jack, Roger Williams, Maysville, and Orange Grove that are worthy of historical investigation from the Black voice. We encourage someone from those communities to take time to research through the local libraries, courthouses, schools, churches and elders. Once the information is compiled, it should be written in a manner wherein the story is told from the voice of the people.

Keep in mind this process may take months and even years to complete. It is, however, critical to be patient, develop appropriate questions, to go wherever is needed to ascertain answers to obtain the mental picture of the history before processing and documentation. To learn, one has to be curious and if curiosity is destroyed, part of the history of any community dies. In essence, Blacks should write about our experiences, simply because THEY have lived THEM!

WHO ARE YOU? We are a population of Black people living in America, the home of the free and the brave. We have formulated everything to have a great culture, then, why not give our race a name and a meaning for totality. I suggest since we are descendents of Africa we are first and foremost African Americans. However, our race is the Black race and, we should be called Black Americans in the land of our birth.

In the beginning, our forefathers' White slave owners provided us with an adopted identity. We were given an adopted first and last name, and a language and culture to use; our body is a composition of genes spewed from many races and has resulted in a rainbow of colors, shades and textures. Some White men told us to return to Africa; but we will not, because we would be `incognito' and in reality, we do not belong there. So who are we? We are Black Americans, born in a place called our Native Land, we have cultivated this land, shed tears of joy and grief when good or bad has happened; and, also, experienced prosperity as well as despair in this land.

We received an education to help plan our livelihood and carry on the fight for liberty, freedom and justice our forefathers died to obtain. We have constructed and erected great buildings and protected this land to keep it free from harm and danger. We also, died during times of peace and war. We were born slaves in this land and freed by its' laws. We were raised Christians and have paid the price for freedom by defending it for one and all. Who are we? We are Black Americans and we have no other homeland except America. We are Americans and we are staking our claim!

Humbling, to say, ``TO GOD BE THE GLORY'', but as Americans we have fallen short of his glory in spite of dying for this land and other privileges. We must remember our Creator is the ruler and maker of ALL things. Because of this, we should know, believe and reap the benefits of this land because it is OURS as long as we live.

'TODAY I STAKE A CLAIM IN MY NATIVE LAND CALLED AMERICA'

Marjorie K. Jones

PART TWO

HISTORICAL PROSPECTIVE

CHAPTER ONE

HISTORICAL PROPECTIVE

BLACK COMMUNITY: MOBILE, ALABAMA

My friend, sister, brothers and I were born with strikes against us from the beginning; because we were born poor and Black in America. We were Mobilians', in the State of Alabama and our place in society was known at an early age. We were taught to stay in our places for no one liked an uppity Black person. Being an uppity (_n_ word) in Mobile, Alabama could lead to negative things happening; and the only person that could help was the White man or the preacher. They could help because of the respect and influence they had in the community. This was the time that powerful hate groups such as the Ku Klux Klan were prevalent. During that period and even today, in some areas of this country it is not what you know, but `who' you know in the political system when trouble occurs.

Even though Blacks experienced discrimination within the Black community, there was a caste system based on skin color, hair texture, professions, money and family name. A few Blacks who had money could buy their way into the so-called Black social upper class society (men only--females were not able to climb the ladder). Blacks who did not have money or fair/light skin were considered lower class and were not allowed to join certain organizations or attend balls, society parties, some weddings, participate in the

5

Black Mardi Gras Coronations or other social functions. Those with the good texture hair and light skin could and would slip into White movie theaters, ride in front of the bus and some even passed for White.

Blacks attended segregated schools and public libraries to further their education. Three of the public high schools and one private Catholic school, respectively, (Dunbar, Central, Mobile County Training and Heart of Mary) are no longer in operation today. Children wore hand-me-downs and homemade clothes or store bought clothes. Additionally, they did not care about name brands, because they were proud just to be able to obtain an education. There was little money so it was difficult to afford riding the bus or eating in the school cafeteria. When money was available many would go to BABES' for a $.10 hot dog with coleslaw and a $.05 soda pop. This famous hot dog stand was located near Central and Heart of Mary High Schools.

Books for school were either purchased from Anders' Book Store—new or used; or from students passing to a higher grade. Lunches were taken in a brown paper bag or lunch box, if you had one. Lunch consisted of cookies, Haas Davis Bologna, or peanut butter and jelly sandwiches. Dinner was the final meal of the day prepared at home by parents, kinfolk or non-kin.

While walking to school, Blacks could get an eye view of the City Dump located in a place called the BOTTOM. In this place, people would sort through the trash for food to ravish whatever they could find. Those people lived in little shanty shacks made from cardboard boxes, or they dug holes in the ground for shelter. This was a way of life in the BOTTOM and one of the sites viewed while walking to school in the 50's.

The Homes of Blacks

Most homes were small but neat and made from wood with little or no grass in the yards; the floors were made of polished hardwood, or covered with linoleum. Floors were mopped once a week with Tide washing powder, Pine Sol, or Lysol; and waxed with Aero Wax using a store bought mop, home made rag mop, hand rags or rags tied to one's feet. A few Blacks owned their homes, others paid to rent: shacks, shot-gunned or double tenant houses for about $10.00 a month. The maintenance of the houses was done by hand to keep them clean, comfortable and livable. For example, lye soap was made and used to scrub floors, clean chairs, tables and clothes, etc.; bluing to brighten clothes before they were ironed with cooked starch--the iron was usually heated on a wood, poker or gas stove/heater. Several Blacks had washing machines with press wringers, others used the old black boiling pot and rub board. There were outdoor toilets with the overhead string for flushing. Front porches were usually bricked half way with wooden steps and contained porch furniture such as: a swing or glider to sit

7

and watch the scenery. In the yards were China Berry and Sycamore trees. Some houses had back garrets with cement or wood steps. In most yards there were vegetable gardens with chicken coupes and homemade barbecue pits. Goats and pigs were raised in the city for food and milk, butter and buttermilk were home churned, ice cream was homemade, and berries were raised and picked for pies and cobblers. The store bought foods were purchased at nominal prices; but because of hard times and limited funds the neighbors shared.

Around most houses, flower gardens were in the front yards with picket fences to keep in the dogs. Most houses had electric lights but kerosene lamps were nearby. For dishwashing, a dishpan of heated water was prepared daily. To drink water, tin cups, coffee mugs or jelly jars were used. Meals were prepared and placed in tin pans or mixed matched China plates. During the week meatless meals were served, however, on Sunday's a full course meal of vegetables, chicken, ham or roast, dessert, with drinks of lemonade, Kool Aid, soda pops, or tea were prepared.

There were no king and queen size beds, only a couch (sofa), full, twin, or rollaway beds. The ceilings were high and walls were covered with wallpaper and knotty pine wood; windows were covered with shades, drapes, curtains or Venetian Blinds. Most homes were furnished with a chest of drawers, hope chest, Chifforobe, rocking chair, radio, clock, calendar, dust or whiskbroom and a hat rack. Doors were unlocked with a door stump to hold it open because people felt safe. However when they decided to leave home a skeleton key was used to lock the door. There were no doorbells, but rather a door rapper. In kitchens, pot bellied stoves and tables adorned with oiled-tablecloths were used. On special holidays, however, linen tablecloths covered the tables. The kitchens also contained small cupboards stacked with special utensils such as the coffee pots and drip grain holder, whistling tea kettles, crank ice cream freezers, churners for butter, rolling pins, graters, file for the knives, mallets, fish scalars, hot plates, strainers, sifters, iron skillets, pie and cake pans, boiling pots, frying pans (old pots and pans were repaired by the tinker man) and rattraps. Most homes did not have televisions until the 1950's and the picture was black and white. Black families watched television while sitting on a couch, sofa, hassock, or the floor. Finally, some families had party line telephones with five-digit access codes.

Most houses had hand made screens with wood window casing and wooden doors. However, there was always a fly squatter and mosquito sprayer filled with gulf oil for insects. There were no air conditioners or central heat, just paper fans, window fans, attic fans, and sweat rags. A few of the homes had iceboxes and every other day people waited for Mr. PeeJo the iceman. The ice cream man, milkman, and vegetable man were also regulars. For hygiene purposes, there were basins, foot tubs, hampers, slop jars; a shaving mug and mop for men, and a douche bag for women— these items were located in the bathroom. The number two (#2) washtub for washing clothes and taking baths was located on the garret. Charcoal and wood were used in the fireplaces for warmth. Stoves and gas heaters were also used for warmth, with tin cans of water on their flat tops to keep moisture in the air. When it was cold, elders would rise early to start the fire in the fireplace, turn off the dripping faucet, and remove the rags wrapped around galvanize pipes that prevented freezing.

Black families with children age(s) of 11 and up were allowed to walk to Downtown to pay utility bills. To get to Downtown it was necessary to walk past the White school that is currently the Mobile County School Board Central Office. While walking to Downtown, children had to remember that grown-ups, including Whites, were addressed as Mr. Mrs. or Miss; and in answering elders on the way, the response was always `yes maam, no maam', or `yes sir, no sir'. It was known that children were to be seen and not heard unless asked to make a comment. If those rules were not followed, the usual consequence was some sort of punishment. Another concern of children was having a spell placed on them for being sassy, eyeballing, staring, and not minding adults.

For misbehaving, most adults could and would chastise neighborhood children.

While walking to Downtown, there were Neon signs, gaslights, street names embossed on cement corner posts and large water mains in the center of paved streets. On arriving Downtown the following stores could be found: Lindys, Goldsteins, Hammels, Metzgers, Gayfers, Raphaels, Lerners, Planters Peanut Shop, Krystals ($.10 burgers) Woolworth, S.H. Kress, Neisners, Walgreens, and Maxey's Formals.

Walking Downtown was not fun, because this was where Black men and women were beaten or harassed by White men for failing to say ``excuse me'' quickly enough for brushing against a White female or failing to answer `yes maam' or `no sir'. This was also the place where Blacks had bus doors shut in their faces. It was understood by Blacks, and never questioned that the back of the bus was the place for them. However, if Whites demanded a seat in the back, it was given even if it required standing until their destination was reached. In one instance, a bus took off with a Black man (my father) whose appearance resembled a White man while his wife (my mother) was not permitted to board because of her dark skin.

Blacks could not own stores Downtown, walk thru or sit in the famed Beinville Square, sit at soda fountains, or shop without being watched by store clerks. Most owners' of stores and salesclerks believed Blacks would steal or did not have money to buy goods on display. There was a nook in some of the stores where Blacks could sit but they had to be mindful of labels and signs such as Colored and White water fountains, and rest rooms. Failure to obey the labels and signs resulted in arrest and unjust sentencing practices, especially if the fines could not be paid.

During segregation, Whites serving jail time were segregated from Blacks and treated better. For example, my father was arrested and placed with the White inmates because they did not know he was a Black man. According to my father, food, bedding, and sanitary conditions were much better where Whites were housed. The aforementioned information was revealed after comparing oral histories with Blacks who served jail time during the 40's, 50's, 60's and 70's.

In addition, in order to become a registered voter in Mobile, Alabama, Blacks had to take and pass a voter registration test administered at the courthouse followed by paying poll taxes. These stipulations to become a registered voter resulted in few obtaining this right.

Blacks were not allowed to get a social security card until the age of 13. It was said, but not documented that the government had a way of segregating races by using the numbers assigned on the social security card. That is, if the two middle digits were even and the year of birth was before 1950 in Mobile, Alabama it was determined you were Black. However, if the two middle digits were odd and the person was born before 1950 it was determined they were White. Another tidbit supposedly used for race identification was a person's last name. For example, some historians stated America's first President George Washington sired children by a Black woman. Because of his shame and disgrace, Whites in the South would not use the sir (last) name of Washington attached to theirs. Public records at the Downtown Courthouse were also separated by race in the local paper.

The doctors' offices and hospitals located near Downtown were segregated with a front door for Whites and a back door for Blacks. Blacks and indigents used the Mobile General Hospital, however, if Whites entered the facilities they were waited on first. Sometimes Blacks spent the day waiting for treatment and in some instances, the wait was in vain.

Persons suffering with Tuberculosis were separated and placed in quarantine at a segregated Tuberculosis hospital located on St. Anthony Street near Downtown. However, because of limited funds, Blacks opted to be treated at home with traditional home remedies. A few of those home remedies are included in Part Three of this book.

Childbirth and Childcare

Along with the Mobile General Hospital and home remedies; midwives were used to bring babies into the world and the birth records were recorded at the State level. Also, families recorded births and other significant records in the family Bible.

The midwives suggested the following: use cloth diapers and rompers. Diapers and rompers were to be washed and hung out to dry with clothespins. Babies were to drink milk mixed with water and Karo syrup or breastfeed. Babies' navels were to be bound with tape to keep them from protruding. It was also a common practice for a penny to be placed around the neck of a baby to denote their year of birth. For teething, gums were to be rubbed with sweet oil to ease the pain. The mother and no one else was allowed to hold the baby for two months because it was believed a baby was defenseless against diseases, and if held during one's menstrual cycle it would cause the strain (diarrhea). New mothers stomachs were to be bound with sheets so they could regain normal waist size and prevent stretch marks. Alum powder was to be used to tighten the vagina after giving birth. A final prevention after childbirth was mothers were to stay in the house at least a month after giving birth, and not wash their hair nor take a full bath during this time.

Conduct in the Community

If a dispute or fight occurred between adults or children, it was called scrapping, clowning or humbugging. These disputes often resulted over name calling, playing the dirty (duz), drinking alcohol, romantic relationships, petty thefts or money debts. Whatever the cause may be, there were hardly any concealed weapons, drug involvement, deadly force or gangs used for enforcement. The closest children came to gang fights was if a person(s) was double-teamed. When and if these disputes or fights occurred, the families and the person(s) involved were labeled as bad, hoodlums, low classed and disgraceful. If women were involved in a fight, it was hard for them to regain respect in the community.

In summary, living during that era was not easy, but we survived because of God, history and the close-knit community. If it were not for God, history and the community, coping with discrimination, segregation and disparity would have been more difficult.

CHAPTER TWO

INFLUENCE OF THE CHURCH——MY FAMILY

The family matriarch was my grandmother and we were not aware of any other relatives. My grandmother cared and provided for my older brother and I. She was a schoolteacher who loved going to church and playing the piano. My grandmother was a religious person who married our step granddaddy. In her own words, he was, she believed below her standards. She would always say, ``Never marry an ignorant man like I did''. My mother, who never left her mother's home, provided and cared for my sister and younger brother. She was an intelligent, proud person who felt life had been harsh; because at 15 years she became pregnant, stopped school and married. Later she married a second time to a man beholding to his mother and who did not want him to marry her because she had been married before and had children. My mother at times tried to live her life through her children, which she later found impossible to do. Our stepfather was abusive but she loved and felt dependent because she had no one else to turn to. Even though my mother may have faltered and we had limited material things, she never lost faith in God. She taught us, to love everybody and most of all God, to stay out of trouble, strive to be somebody and eventually everything would be all right.

Every Sunday my grandmother and mother let us walk to church in our Sunday frock. We were Christian Methodist by faith. On our way to Sunday school, our teacher would call us by nicknames and the children in the neighborhood would form a line and follow her to the church. During Sunday school, children were taught the golden rule, the importance of sharing, caring, giving and how Jesus loved and died for us. They also taught us how skin color had nothing to do with his love for us and that God is the father of mankind.

We loved to listen to gospels and hymns; and we sang songs made famous by Mahalia Jackson, Dorothy Norwood, Albertina Walker, Clay Evans, Shirley Caesar, C.L. Franklin, Mighty Clouds of Joy, and the Gospel Keynotes. The nickel or dime for Sunday school was tied in the girls' hankies and the boys' money was kept in their pants' pocket. After Sunday school we attended Sunday Church where we learned the wonders and miracles of God such as: --all things are possible if you believe--there is always hope in desperate situations—and God will take care of you if you believe. We learned that Jesus, God's Son, loved little children and he died for our sins. We were also taught, we are here for a short time so we must obey God, glorify Him for his goodness and when our task is finished, we would go to Heaven. Our Sunday school teacher and preacher stressed we must remember, ``If God was not known and we did not have Him to lean on, times would be difficult''. We learned if we followed these teachings, we would be with God and his Son, Jesus, forever. These teachings gave us hope and the incentive to reach goals beyond our years, but most of all to dream of a bright future.

The church family held the following activities: Penny Fairs, Coronations, teas, Women and Men Day, cookouts, and bake sales with funds going to the Stewards and Trustees for church expenses. These affairs helped us to understand God loves a `Cheerful Giver.' The activities listed below were also a part of the church agenda: dinners, weddings, Easter, Christmas, school programs and wakes. Finally, there were families who held wakes services (viewing of the deceased) in their living rooms instead of the church.

CHAPTER THREE

LIFESTYLES OF BLACKS DURING THE 1940'S, 50'S, 60'S & 70'S

THE LIFESTYLE OF BLACK WOMEN IN MOBILE, ALABAMA   40'S——70'S

Employment

During the week, Black women worked or traveled around with MISS ANN, a common name for rich White women, in white uniforms, cotton stockings, aprons, and hairnets; worked on jobs such as florist, cooks, maids, laundry workers, dish washers, beauticians, or seamstresses (few were professionals). The pay was menial and usually kept in the bosom, hidden, or buried.

Activities and Livelihood

The women who stayed at home would listen to the rain at times on the tin top roofs as they cooked over pot-bellied stoves or made fires in the fireplace in a shot gunned, double tenant or rooming houses, made weekly grocery lists, kept accounts of bills, cleaned, bored ears and made earrings, knitted, gossiped ``chewed the fat'' while dipping snuff, made wicker or straw baskets and hats, ironed, quilted, designed various kinds of needlework, and shaped dollies using soda bottles as a model to make them stand. When the dollies were shaped, they were placed on coffee tables, whatnot stands, or settees. Along with these activities, the women also taught family values to the children. Most Black women had common names and were usually called Mrs., Miss, Big Mama, honey, sugar, Ma-Dear, Miss fine, nanna, toosie, tittie or girl; the children's names were also common with the girls' middle name being Mae, Lou, Ann or Jean and the boys' middle name usually being Lee.

Foods and Leisure Dress

Some of the foods and drinks prepared, preserved and distilled were hog head cheese, souse, smoked meats, deer sausage, cakes, soups, gumbo, skinned soaked and cooked wild meats, butter, pies, preserves, canned vegetables, cane sugar, cobblers, puddings, tea cakes, short bread, hoecakes, flap jacks, sorghum, honey from honey combs, wine, whiskey, and homebrew. While the women prepared and preserved foods, they would snack on sardines & crackers, hoop cheese & coffee rolls, raw oysters & crackers, fat back, sorghum and biscuits, starch, clay dirt or sugar cane. The usual attire worn around the house were the following: head rags, scarves, or hair net over paper rollers, bobby pinned hair, housedresses, housecoats covered by aprons, socks, cotton support stockings, house shoes or slides.

Styles for Black Women

For a late evening outing or Sunday affair, Black women attire was a hairdo in an upsweep, bob with a V-neck and tint, crimp curls, rat pad, chignon, French roll and bangs, pageboy, press and curl with hot oil, or pompadour. Dresses were made from Taffeta, prints, plaids, chiffon, sequins, organza, lace, nylon, polyester, broad cloth and strips, flannel, tweed, corduroy, suede, velvet, mohair, wool, file, seer-sucker, or plain cotton material. The style of dress included: sundresses, fish tail, scalloped, chemise, pantsuits, tunics, two-piece suits with dickeys, snap collars, turtlenecks, V-necks and blouses with skirts which were A-line, gathered, flair or tight—hemlines at mid calf. A corset, waist cincher, or girdle was used for a body foundation and most women wore wide brim or pillbox hats or a sporty tam.

Women accented their looks with large hoop earrings, nut-brown powder, rouge, nail polish, jeweled accessories, perfume, and red lipstick. A smiling face would often reveal an open-face gold crown, a work of dentistry popular during that era. A snazzy dresser would also wear shaded glasses, red-fox stockings with back seams; garters or garter belt, boots, spike heels or pumps and a colorful parasol. Some women carried a purse that usually contained a cigarette holder, fan, handkerchief, and gloves. During inclement weather, a person would wear a topper, casual or swing coat, stoll, cape, P-coat, comforter, car-coat, leather or suede trench coat, sweater, cloak, fur-trim overcoat or a fox or rabbit fur, head scarf, or shawl.

THE LIFESTYLE OF BLACK MEN IN MOBILE, ALABAMA   40'S——70'S

Employment

Men were the head of the family and chief provider. Many were merchant seaman, porters on segregated trains, night watchmen, worked on or at the banana boat wharf, tug boats, state docks, shoe shops, vegetable stands, picked cotton, potatoes or pecans in Baldwin County, Alabama, hunted for food, barbers, made bean bags/furniture, upholstery; butchers, chauffeurs, garbage collectors, busboys, laborers, tailors, morticians, painters, or personally worked for Mr. Charlie, the rich White man, for menial pay. Blacks were at the bottom of the wage scale and the jobs were referred to as not being worth two bits. The pay scale ranged from $.65 an hour to $1.15 with a week's work usually consisting of 40 hours. The only hope for Blacks was to receive Social Security after working 40+ years and/or turning 62 years old. The dress wear for work or home was long johns, over/cover-alls, old britches, sweat rags/hats/caps, socks, work boots or sneakers.

Activities and Livelihood

Some men enjoyed bicycling, shooting pool, standing by storefronts to gossip, fishing, hunting, shooting crap, singing in quartets with guitar music and harmonicas, making moonshine, homebrew or wine; working as a shade tree mechanic, playing crochet, lollygagging, playing cards, dominoes, pinochle, playing the lottery, having cold brews

22

or suds at the local bar. Some of the common nicknames for men were: honey do, sweetie pie, sugar daddy, big daddy, bubba, baby, papa, poppa, paw paw, paw, da, daddy, granddaddy, plenty money, cool, cool breeze, fat daddy, and daddy cool.

Styles for Men

Evening or Sunday hairdo for men was called a Process, which was hair slicked down with lots of grease, jell or a conk solution. The haircuts consisted of flattops, cue balls, crew cuts, or fair daddy and in the 60's an Afro. Face pampering included trimming the mustache, sideburns, goatee, beard or a shave. The open-faced gold crown dental work was very popular for men. Most men sported Apple Jacks, Kangos, beanies or skullcaps; stingy brims, felts, stove tops, Beavers, or Russian hats. Men would dress up in sport coats and pants; trey or double breast pin stripped or solid suits with a vest, belts, suspenders, jive/watch chain, or rabbit foot. The style of shirt included T-Shirt, Dashiki or dress shirt with cuffs and tie. Men carried a handkerchief, gloves, or walking cane, accented with a tamp walk. Men wore cologne, shade glasses, flashy jewelry, spit shinned Stacy Adams, lizard, alligator, hushpuppies or Floorshiem shoes, with fancy socks. Inclement weather attire was long wool, suede, or leather fur trimmed topcoats; chesterfields, cashmere sweaters, capes, dickeys, pull over s shawls, cloaks, comforters or trench coats.

Employment

Some of the children, with parental permission, traveled to Baldwin County, Alabama to pick pecans, potatoes, or cotton; babysat, housecleaned, sold newspapers, distributed weekly ads, sold bottles, cut lawns, carried float banners, or worked as delivery boys for menial pay.

Activities and Livelihood

Activities for the children included walking to Malbis or Pollman's Bakery shops to purchase goodies or sweets, visiting vegetable stands; playing games, attending rock and roll shows, attending school functions, and going to the Harlem or Saenger theater (Blacks had to sit in the balcony at the Saenger). Other activities included reading and listening to ghost stories around large barrels of burning wood used to smoke off mosquitoes, attending football games, going to the circus and fair, fishing, shooting marbles, watching television, hanging out with cut buddies, flying kites, playing with homemade toys, listening to the neighbors play the guitar, playing football and softball in the White Magnolia Cemetery for a contest game held in Maysville on Friday nights. These contest games gave the children an opportunity to go to the Bee Bop Teen Club and dance after the game. Finally going to the local ice-cream parlor for a float, hanging out at teenage clubs like Dennis and Marcella's to dance, and figure skate in the streets.

24

These are merely a few of the activities children innocently enjoyed.

Styles for Girls

The Sunday or evening attire included: prints, calico, nylon, pinfold, chemise or sun-back dresses with T-straps, ruffles, skirts and blouses, jumpers, bloomers, petticoats, hip or can-can slips and tights. The hairstyles consisted of: French rolls, twists, Shirley Temple curls with halo bands; braids, plaits, pigtails, or bangs and ponytails clasped with ribbons, rubber bands, or barrettes. Hair styles also included pressed hair with Blue Magic, Royal Crown, Sulfur Aide, Moroline, or Wylon hair grease. The style of shoes included: loafers, Buster Browns, sandals, hush puppies, pumps or two-toned oxfords with dress socks. The jewelries worn were bangles, necklaces, anklets, bracelets, pearls and/or earrings. Inclement weather attire included: parasols, car-coats, toppers or swing back coats and gloves. On special occasions hats and tams were worn.

Styles for Boys

The boys' attire included trey or double-breasted solid or pin stripped suits. Others wore sport coats with pants, shirts and ties, Ivy League pullovers and V-Neck sweaters. They also wore Penny Loafers or Buster Brown Oxford shoes with socks. Sometimes hats, beanies, caps, topcoats and gloves were worn depending on the weather. To complete the well-groomed look, a fresh haircut was the norm.

Culture, Customs and Discipline

Included in the Black culture was a sense of pride and respect for self and community. From that reference point the man was considered head of the household, which meant he provided money for food, clothes and shelter. Most Black women and children did as he directed and everything was ready and prepared when he came home. The women were responsible for everything pertaining to the well being of the family and management of the home. This custom still exist today in some Black families.

If the family owned a car, it was usually a Cadillac for status or a rag top convertible of some sort. The price of gasoline was $.15 or $.20 cent a gallon, which meant gas was affordable and you could ride for long periods of time while spending little.

Clothes and dress had an implied status in the Black community and it was important to be a sassy and snazzy dresser. The color of clothes was important because loud bold colors implied country or hick. If men wore red, pink, yellow or purple they were not seen as masculine. The boys on the other hand wore long dark dress pants to school and the girls wore colorful dresses. When the children returned from school they would change into play clothes, tennis shoes or in some cases bare feet.

Little girls who played with boys, or with boys' toys were called tomboys and little boys who played with girls or

with girls' toys were called weak and girlish. Most upper
class children were labeled as stuck-up or Miss goody-goody
two shoes. Children labeled as tattled tails or crybabies
were scorned and ridiculed by peers. In spite of these
descriptions, when dusk dark approached, children in the
neighborhood were accounted for. They were expected to be
at home completing chores, doing homework or preparing for
dinner.

Children were expected to obey parents, teachers and
adults. They watched television with parents because the
shows were family oriented with no profanity, heavy
lovemaking and nudity was not shown or expressed. Some of
the shows viewed were: Howdy Doody, Mickey Mouse, American
Bandstand, Ted Mack, Little Rascals, cartoons, Ed Sullivan,
Jack Benny, Groucho Mark, Red Skeleton, Roy Rogers, Wild
Bill, Gene Autry, Bonanza, Annie Oakley, Loretta Young and
the Amos n' Andy Show.

<u>Mental and Physical Discipline</u>

Children and adults alike wore ID tags called dog
chains for identification purposes. If children or grown-
ups were mentally ill, they were sent to Searcy Hospital in
Mount Vernon, Alabama. If children were uncontrollable or
truant, they were sent to the ``The Detention Home on Davis
Avenue or to Mount Meigs, a state operated school. When
they returned from a state school, teeth were usually
missing in the front to display status. Adults who broke

the law were sent to jail, prison farm or penitentiary. Finally, elders who could not provide for themselves had to be placed in the Old Folks Home by family or other state officials.

Coupled with the livelihood, dress, activities, mental and physical discipline of the women, men, and children, the family's name and background was also important. If pregnancy occurred, especially if one was a student or single, it was considered a disgrace. A pregnant girl could not attend school and the rule was to beg forgiveness in front of the church congregation. A child could not be put in the father's name unless there was a marriage. If a boy or girl was seen kissing or showing affection, the girl was downgraded and called fast, hussy or heifer. Girls could date one boy and the family had to know his background—the usual dating age was (17) and a young lady could not stay out past 10 p.m. If there was going to be a formal wedding, the young man had to ask the father's permission followed by preparation for the wedding with the traditional white gown. In some families, if a girl became pregnant and not married, the two were forced to have what was called a ``shot gunned wedding''.

Family planning and birth control pills were not common, so many babies were conceived and born; however, locally, illegal abortions were performed. Overweight children were rarely seen, however, there were other problems and deformities. Those conditions could have been corrected if babies were born in hospitals and proper diets were followed during pregnancies. It was commonly spoken and believed by some Black men, ``if you want to control your woman, keep her barefoot and pregnant''. This practice along with the lack of money for hygiene made it difficult for some women to develop positive self esteem.

In light of low self-esteem, single men wooed the attention of available unmarried women with wolf whistling, winking the eye, flowers or through family matchmaking. The single men and boys also used a hand jive language, talked jive talk, and whistling as a way to communicate messages. The young ladies would let them know they were interested by giving them the eye, wearing a flower over their left ear, or by dropping a handkerchief for the eligible young man to retrieve and return.

Money Shortages

There were numerous Black men who did not know how to avoid loan sharks, because they could not read or write. Sometimes their boss would loan them money until payday and then require payment at 100 percent plus interest. This type of arrangement allowed for little or no money at the end of the week. Failure to have enough money resulted in the loss of cars, furniture, homes, and finally their credit. Limited knowledge relating to finances meant Blacks were not able to save money and they also had limited trust in banks. However, by the 50's Blacks began to acquire professional jobs, even though limited in number; and changes began to take place. Professions included: merchant marines, armed services where Blacks slept in separate rooms, mingled and ate in dining halls with Whites only to return to a segregated civilian life. During the war years it was mandatory through a draft, that Blacks enter the service. Other professions pursued were: nurses, teachers, federal government jobs at Brookley Field Air Force Base, dentists, entrepreneurs, morticians, doctors and preachers.

Adult Entertainment and Music

Blacks in Mobile, Alabama waited for Fridays' when the eagles flew (had money) so they could walk to the back street (go out) to have a good time. Some entertainment places for grown-ups were night clubs, Black theaters such as the Ace, Harlem, Pike, and Lincoln; The ILA Hall Ballroom for balls for the upper-class Blacks, Fort Whiting Auditorium for shows, a few restaurants and back yard cafes such as Pope's, Velma's, Frazier's, Dragon's, CIO, Ella's Barbecue, and Lockette's. Blacks could also visit the six Black beaches: Mon Luis Island, Roger Thomas, Alexander Lake, Chestang, Edge Water, and Paradise. There was the Bay Breeze Social Club, the Black Folks' juke joints/dives, or the Honky Tonks clubs for adult entertainment shows. These

Honky Tonks were located on every corner in the Red Light District Down-The Bay and Cross Town.

The jukes joints had wooden floors, dingy lights, a crude bar with tables/chairs and booths. The Blues, local bands, piano playing, quartets, Jitter Bug, Boogie Woogie, and Jazz music would ring from the doors of the juke joints. In the juke joints the guitar and harmonic music by artist such as: Jimmie Reed, Nancy Wilson, Howling Wolf, Peg Leg Bates, The Treniers', Roy Hamilton, Pig Meat Marcum, Mom Mabley, Jimmy Lynch, Sammy Davis, Jr., Little Ester, Red Foxx, Johnny Ace, Mills' Brothers, Pearl Bailey, Lionel Hamilton, Miles Davis, Quincy Jones, Charles Brown and Little Milton were heard. Additional artists were: Guitar Slim, Muddy Waters, John Coltrane, Johnny Ace, B.B. King, Bobby Bland, Louis Armstrong, Count Basie, Al Green, Jimmy Witherspoon, Lionel Hamilton, Elmo James, Dinah Washington, Nappy Brown, Rosco Gordon, Robert Johnson, Bobby Rush, Robert Belfour, Big Mae Bell, Bill Doggett, Lightning Hawking, and Big Joe Turner could be heard until 2 a.m. nightly.

Some of the dances included: the camel walk, grind, applejack, hambone, Charleston, Be Bop, ball & jack, two step, the nasty, tremble, shake, stump, Huckle Buck, the dog, mash potatoes, jerk and the swing. The music during this era was played on radios, jukebox, Rock Colas, turntables, or the phonograph. Record sizes were 45, 33 1/3 or 78 rpm. Blacks enjoyed going to the juke joints to

mingle with friends, dance, listen to music, drink soft
drinks, wine or beer; and smoke cigarettes. The choices of
drinks included: Red Dagger, Mogen David, Silver Satin,
Thunderbird, Boones Farms, or Riunite wines, Tequila,
whiskey, scotch, rum, gin, vodka, and Draft beer could be
purchased by the pitcher or mug. Twenty Grand, Miller and
Falstaff beer could be purchased for $.15 cents a bottle.
Chesterfield, Viceroy, Marlboro, Camel, Pall Mall and Lucky
Strike cigarettes were $.20 a pack with free matches. Soft
drinks such as: Nehi, Seven-Up, Russ, Cokes, and Royal
Crown, (belly washer) were also available. Garret snuff,
Red Man chewing tobacco, smoking pipes, Tampa Nuggets cigars
along with Spearmint, Peppermint, Juicy Fruit, and Double
mint chewing gum were plentiful. It was commonly said by
Blacks' to one another' `` Boy, if you could be Black on
Friday Nights' and the weekends', you'd never want to be
White no more''.

Young Adults Music and Dance

The young adults and children were fans of rock and roll
and listened to tunes and music by artist such as: Little
Willie John, Frankie Lyman, Smokey Robinson, Ted Taylor,
Johnny Taylor, Millie Jackson, Betty Wright, Carla Thomas,
Johnny Mathis, Cissy Houston, Gladys Knight, Ramsey Lewis,
Aretha Franklin, Patty Labelle, Temptations, O-Jays, Little
Milton, Impressions, Brook Benton, Five Satins, Sam Cooke,
Coasters, Be-Gees, Otis Redding, Joe Simon, Fats Domino,

Little Richard, Chuck Jackson, Chuck Willis, Chuck Berry, Jackie Wilson, Little Anthony and the Imperials, Mary Wells, The Mid-Nighters, Clyde McPhatter, Martha Reaves, The Supremes, Mary Wells, James Brown, Joe Hinton, Ike and Tina Turner, Gene Chandler, The Dells, Baby Cortez, Z.Z. Hill, Johnny Mathis, Ruth Brown, Etta James, Theola Kilgore, Bobby Womack, The Dells, The Drifters, Jerry Butler, Bobby Womack, Nancy Wilson, Ben E. King, Chantels, Carla Thomas, Rufus Thomas, The Staple Singers, Peaches & Herb, Marvin Gaye and Ray Charles. This era was considered the Doo Wop days. The dances during this period were: the grind, the two-step, Cha Cha Cha, hand jive, The James Brown, camel walk, nitty gritty, pop eye, monkey, swim, jerk, the dog, tremble, float, bump, hoochie coochie, hulley gulley, the chicken, continental, Madison, Charleston, hambone, swing, fast, the strut, slow, limbo and the twist.

CHAPTER FOUR

DISPARITY AMONG SOME BLACKS LEAD TO HIGHER ACHIEVEMENTS:

The feeling of disparity and little money to make ends meet stimulated the development of goals and dreams among Blacks.

Private enterprises were afraid to hire Blacks because it was bad for business. There were one or two businesses that hired Blacks, but most were either over qualified, received less pay or had to train Whites to be their supervisor. Usually, Blacks performed the work of two or three persons or had to look White to obtain the job.

The opportunity to purchase a home or be a landowner was difficult because of limited funds, bad credit, and strict bank and mortgage requirements in order to qualify for a loan. In certain neighborhoods Blacks could not buy or rent homes even if they had the money because of Redlining.

My family was one the few who owned property in the area, but it was not to our advantage. Shortly after the death of my grandmother in 1961, my step-grandfather asked us to leave the homestead because of his interest in other women. However, I never forgot my grandmother and 41 years later in 2002, I kept a promise by placing a marker on her grave.

My brother, Emrich, graduated high school in 1959, attended college for one year and served in the armed service for 20 years.   He married twice and is the father of 10 children.   To date he has (14) grandchildren and is employed with the Corps of Engineers in Mobile, Alabama.

I graduated from high school in 1961 the year my grandmother died and entered The Branch, a two-year college, in Mobile, Alabama. After graduation, I completed the Bachelor of Science Degree at Alabama State Teachers' College in Montgomery, Alabama. While there, I lived on an allowance of $5.00 a week, a meager allowance for clothes and food.   For solace, my pet was a gold fish, however, it bubbled too much for my landlord and was later discarded. Due to my meager allowance, there was no money for textbooks—so remembering what was taught in class was very important.

In spite of the pressures of college and a determination to graduate, I participated in the Civil Rights demonstrations. During these experiences I was forced to lie down in the street, along with others, by mounted police in the middle of Downtown, Montgomery, Alabama.   One high-note, in spite of the brutal police, students were marching, touching, seeing, hearing and participating in Dr. Martin Luther King's ``I have a Dream Speech and March on the Capitol.   Dr. King, a short, medium built man with a dynamic speaking voice made me feel like I could conquer the world. I graduated in 1965 but did not participate in the ceremony due to limited funds for expenses.

My initial teaching position was in Marengo County, in Linden, Alabama. It was alleged the superintendent of public schools was an active member of the Ku Klux Klan and I was advised to say beforehand, `Yes Sir, Mr.▒--- Sir' periodically during the interview. The teaching position paid $300.00 a month. Most of this money was sent to my mother because she needed it most. After working for several months, I found this county to be one of the most racist places I had ever encountered. Blacks had to enter through back doors in 1967 and address Whites as Mr. and Mrs.. The social clubs, businesses and doctors offices had nice seating and decor for Whites with a nook in the back for Blacks; there were cotton fields, old plantations, wading pools, chickens, cows, and horses found on school properties; with few inside toilets and running water in the Black communities.

The family I rented a room from, son was arrested for allegedly showing his private part to a White woman. On the same night of the arrest, the city leaders and the Ku Klux Klan met at a local store. After the meeting, they came to the house on horses to tell the landlord to come to the store. At the meeting they said his son could get out of jail if he used the deed to his land for bail. He decided to give them the deed, but still feared for his son's safety because of the Ku Klux Klan. Two nights later after the meeting, a friend from Montgomery, Alabama put the 16 year old in the trunk of his car and transported him North. His mother was grief stricken, but due to threats against his life, she also knew he could never return. In spite of owning the land, when his son did not appear for trial, the land was taken and the bond revoked. I decided to leave after that school year literally running back to Mobile, Alabama never to return or live there again.

Finally, after teaching for several years, I obtained a Masters in Supervision and Education from Alabama State University in 1975. After teaching in the business field at the high school level for 32 years, I decided to retire in 1997. I have been married twice and have one son, Eddie, who is pending graduation from Alabama & College, Huntsville, Alabama; raised a nephew, Carl who is a teacher and coach in the Mobile County School system; and have one grandson, Micah Caleb who is 5 years old.

My sister, Cherryl graduated from high school in 1964. She married four times and is the mother of three children and eight grandchildren. She attended college for two years, worked at the Mobile County Health Department for 25 years and retired in 1999.

Finally, my brother, Clifton, finished high school while in the Armed Service. After a tour of duty in the service, he moved to North Carolina and worked as a linesman. He was one of the first Black's in North Carolina to work as a telephone linesman, however, 1972 he was killed in an automobile accident. I am humbled by my family's accomplishments and believe we are endowed with God's gifts to use on His behalf.

There is a simple formula given to me through meditation as an inspiration to inspire those who want to attain economic stability and success. This formula stresses setting priorities in life by considering the following: (a) MONEY, FAMILY, LIFESTYLE, and CAREER: Second, (b) Establish career goals and choices in life; (c) Third, decide the level of education needed to attain these choices, goals and salaries. (d) Fourth, determine what college, technical/ trade school, or armed service can provide the best curriculum and career choice. (e) Fifth, determine likes, dislikes, and job interests. (f) Sixth, develop a budget to ensure economic stability.

CHAPTER FIVE

DOWN-THE-BAY

The Down-The-Bay area obtained its' name because of its location near the Mobile Bay. This area was bound on the North by Government Street, South by North Carolina Street, West by the Mobile Bay, and on the East by Broad Street. Living Down-The-Bay was great not only because families greeted each other with hugs and a show of love; but there was a sense of pride and unity. The young men defended this area by not allowing outsiders entrance. Basically, everyone knew and looked out for one another. If people decided to leave the area, they would return to see the home folks on special days. If a person died and was from the Bay area, everybody attended the funeral--this trend continues today. A black ribbon was placed on the front door and adult family members would mourn the death of a love one for a month by wearing the color black; also, there was limited social contact for about six months.

It was nothing like living Down-The-Bay. Families lived from day to day and for payday on Friday. They owned a car if they could afford it and some had a few nice clothes. Basically, this was a predominately Black area with relatively few Whites. In fact, in Mobile, Alabama the population was Black, White, or Creole with no foreigners. Also there were streets, roads, gutters, and alleys but no one-way signs. The streets were made of dirt, concrete, and cobblestone with gas or light poles. Door to door salesmen were visible; and milk, laundry, and prescriptions were picked up and delivered.

In the early 40's and 50's there were no Blacks in city government. Children were usually home by nightfall and they did not own cars or motorbikes. The 5:30 p.m. news was the big event in the evenings and, in particular, the weather forecast. The weather was important because of thunderstorms and the possibility of hurricanes during hurricane season. If people in the Bay area heard warnings of pending bad weather, homes, windows and buildings were boarded up and everyone would sit, lie down, or be quiet until the storm was over. The scripture reading that explained this action was: ``But The Lord Is In His Holy Temple: Let All The Earth Keep Silent Before Him'' (Habakkuk 2:20)

The Bay area also produced famous and prominent people such as: Sachel Paige, Amos Otis and Willie McCovery, the baseball players. This is where Birdie Mae Davis lived, the first Black to attend an all-White public school. The Birdie Mae Davis Civil Rights Case was resolved in the early 90's; also Vivian Malone, the first Black to enter the University of Alabama during the 60's. Others from the Bay are: Alexander Herman, businessman and father of Alexis Herman, Secretary of Labor under President Clinton; Dr.

James Gavin, President of Morehouse School of Medicine as of July 1, 2002; Dr. W. Russell, Dr. E.B. Goode, Charles Black-ledge, PHD, Creola Gibby and Phillip Leslie, attorneys; Lamont Godwin, international banker; Bob Brazier, first Black newscaster; Percy Mauldin, first Black Radio announcer; Clinton Johnson, Mobile City Councilman; Gary Cooper Sr., businessman; A.J. Cooper, first Black Mayor of Prichard, AL; his brother Gary Cooper Jr., past Ambassador to Jamaica and retired Brigadier General; and Dr. Leon Howard, past president of Alabama State University.

The first Black newspapers were printed Down-The-Bay (The Mobile Review, Mobile Beacon and the Telegram). Crime was scarce Down-The-Bay, however, a few people illegally sold shinny (corn liquor, white lightning), homebrew, ran Crap/Hit/Skin houses, smoked dope and sold lottery tickets. The area also had the first Black firemen and policemen to patrol in the 50's. One of those policemen was my stepfather, Clifton Aaron Sr.. Aaron walked a beat in the Bay area armed with a Billy club, whip and gun. However, Black policemen could not arrest Whites or drive the black and white police cars. Blacks could not ride in White cabs, so a Black owned City Cab Company was formed. The first and largest grocery stores were founded in the Bay area (Delchamps and Namans). Other business establishments were the 7-Up Bottling Company, NewBold's, Cox, Laden and Parker Drug Stores; Irby's, Utees, and Lee Etta's Beauty Saloons,

Ice Cream Parlor, Dairy Queen, New Orleans Furniture Store, Leon Dry Good, Bay & Gulf, Miss Margie's, Juzangs, Boykins, and Mr. Few' grocery stores; Chin Laundry, Marcella's and Dennis Teenage Shops, and the Harlem Theater where children would harass Dead Man, the floorwalker. The movie pictures were Black and White, Cinema Scope, Technicolor, or 3D on film reel. There were other non-profit places the people of the Bay used for social gatherings, oratorical contests, and performances such as the Saw Mill Union Hall and Big Zion A.M.E. Zion Church.

A prominent part of the Down-the-Bay area, which would be difficult for one to forget was the jukes joints and chicken shacks such as the Spider's Inn, CIO, Toast Of The Town, Talk of the Town, The Night Hawk, Brown Derby, Dragon Club, Club Rumba, Top Hat, Green Pastures, Tin Top, Hummingbird, I-10, The Silver Slipper, and Velma's and Popes Restaurants. Another place the children in the neighborhood would frequent illegally was West Tavern where they could dance, smoke cigarettes and act like grownups.

Some other creative events was watching a man called Hot Foot Sam entertaining on the corner of Cedar & Texas, people clowning around or sitting under the big tent during the 50's to hear Little Richard preach the gospel. Others would visit Floyd Bolar's Shoe Shop or Brown Skin's Shoe Shine Parlor. Noon's and Pugger's Barber Shops were where the men met to gossip. Some even had fun reading the Mobile

Beacon also called the intellectual paper that discussed neighborhood news. On Saturdays', there were Down-The-Bay fish fries on the corner of Texas and Warren Street with a menu of popeyed mullet, homemade ice cream and cake. Men and women would stand and sing on street corners (Doo Wop songs), while others whistled the tunes. The general feelings then were of love, safety and security.

There were school dances such as: waist dances (fee for your entrance was your waist measurement), birthday parties where the grind, swing, jitterbug, and rock and roll were danced. If the weather was pleasant, one would dance and dream about love, future goals and aspirations under the stars. On those special nights, hip slips, hoops, or can cans with poodle skirts, bobby socks and tennis shoes were the attire.

Holidays were fun with May Days' and the King and Queen's Coronation at Council and Emerson Schools where many goodies, games, and activities were offered. Thanksgiving Day consisted of a Turkey Day football game between Central High and Mobile County Training School, with the culmination of a turkey dinner with family and friends. Halloween was fun too, when children wore homemade costumes and went door to door where the front porch lights were on to obtain treats; and if treats were not given soda pop tops and water balloons were thrown at the house.

On Christmas day there was singing, parties, and family dinners. The dinners included ham, turkey, gumbo, vegetables, macaroni & cheese, cakes (fruit cake was a favorite), candies, nuts, fruits, Egg Nog and Mogen David Wine. Mistletoe was found over door entrances to receive kisses from friends. On this day children wore new clothes, shoes and jewelry. Small children received toys and older children received skates and money. For Christmas, Selma Street and Texas Hill was where everyone skated. The children and grown-ups then could skate better than some professional skaters of today.

Fourth of July celebration consisted of children and grown-ups shooting fireworks and playing games. On New Year's Eve, parties were a must to celebrate the beginning of a New Year. New Year's was also celebrated by praying, making resolutions, singing the song Auld Lang Syne, going to church or firing guns/fireworks at midnight. The New Year's dinner consisted of Black Eye Peas cooked with ham hocks and a dime for good luck; greens for money and hog jowls/chitterlings for prosperity and longevity, seafood, barbecue and watermelon.

Mardi Gras consisted of festivals, balls, parades, and eating the King & Queen cake to see who would get the plastic baby embedded inside. Whoever found the plastic baby was responsible for baking a cake for the next event. This

custom was practiced throughout the two-weeks of Mardi Gras.
Watching the mollies dressed in costumes walking down Texas
Street (the main drag) doing their thing was also exciting.
Those were the hay days of Down-The-Bay that culminated with
Easter, the celebration of the Resurrection of Christ. The
children had Easter egg hunts on Saturday with an Easter
Parade on Sunday where they strutted down the Texas Street.
Another reason for the children strutting down Texas was the
start of Vacation Bible School that originated Down-The-Bay
by a White minister named Reverend Monroe.

Those were great times, but in the early 1960's the
City government initiated a plan to take control of the
Down-The-Bay community through a federal program called
Urban Renewal and a process called Eminent Domain. The
people were devastated by this decision. There were other
areas the City could have revitalized, why did they choose
Down-The-Bay? It was speculated that Whites and the City of
Mobile wanted the LAND for personal reasons and for its'
location near Downtown Mobile--since this was a Black
community, Whites could not make money. Another concern was
Whites did not have access to the land and could not take it
directly. Also the large concentration of Blacks was
perceived as a threat, because Whites felt they could not
frequent the community at will. Finally, they could not
control nor could they scare them with Ku Klux Klan tactics.

45

There was rarely a reason to leave the community because most everything was in walking distance. A feeling of security existed and it was a city with its own culture, pride and roots. The primary reasons to leave was to shop Downtown, attend high school, work and after death, the cemetery. The church bells would toll when someone died or on the day of a funeral.

When the land was taken, landowners were not compensated fairly. Families were uprooted and displaced (some news articles to this effect are found in this book) and nothing could be done to stop this madness when the demolition machines and work teams started clearing the area. To this day, some of the city's planning and constructions for the Down-The-Bay area has never materialized such as schools and shopping centers.

Finally, after 20 years the land was resold at a much higher price to White real estate companies and businesses. Whites began to open new businesses and frequent the area as never before. When a group of former Down-The-Bay residents tried to sue the city in 1985 to regain the land, they were told the statue of limitation had run out and it was to late to take legal action.

My family relocated to Toulminville an area a few miles from Down-The-Bay in 1963. Years after that move, I began to yearn for the closeness and family atmosphere of the Bay, but it was to no avail. About this time (1991), my younger brother, stepfather, and beloved mother had died. After my mother's death, I was desolate and needed someone older to confide in such as an aunt, uncle, or cousin. Because of this, I began to search for immediate family and kinfolk. My brother, Emrich, had been searching as well and subsequently made contact with our biological father while stationed in Texas. That contact enabled him to obtain the phone number of an aunt who lived in Chicago, Illinois. After contacting her it was evident she did not know much about her mother, grandfather, and grandmother who had lived in Claiborne, Alabama; but we were told of a great-grandfather, named Henry Robinson. From here the decision was made to travel to Claiborne, Alabama where it was discovered this was once a thriving city. While there, we met a man who directed us to the sister of our great-grandfather, Henry Robinson. Aunt Carol, Henry's 100+ years old sister, told us the family size, names, and that Henry Robinson had been a wealthy landowner. From the family history it was also noted the family in Claiborne knew of the grandchildren and great-grandchildren, but did not know how to locate them.

However, the extended family thought on another visit, we were interested in the land and not the family heritage. While conversing, they began to realize we were merely looking to fill a void. It was after numerous conversations, we learned the patriarch of the family, Armstead Jackson had 3 wives and 22 children. My great-great-grand-mother was his first wife (Darkus, a Native American Indian) and mother of 6 children. Henry Robinson was the first-born of Darkus and the stepson of Armstead Jackson. Henry was a servant, as was his real father, Henry Sr.--they lived on the land of James Macon in Clark County, Alabama in the 1880's. He married and had 3 children with my great-grandmother, Margaret and a child, Virginia by another woman. Unfortunately, Henry, my great-grand mother, and their children are deceased. The only living relatives are Virginia, a daughter and Gladys, a granddaughter. After talking with Virginia and others, I was given a family reunion book that contained the family tree and pictures, met a cousin in 1993 and obtained additional information. The next year while visiting in Chicago, Illinois I met aunt Gladys; shortly afterwards, Aunt Virginia came to Mobile, Alabama for a visit. It was during that visit, a more detailed history of the family and information about her father, his land and what happened to it was obtained.

This is where the story of cheating and stealing of Black owned land in Monroe and Clark Counties began to materialize. Acquisitions of oral histories have caused speculations that in the South, Blacks were given 40 acres and a mule by the Federal Government; but some courthouses containing these records of Wills and deeds, mortgages and other transactions were destroyed by fire.   It is also speculated that Blacks were taken advantage of because they were illiterate and did not understand what they were signing by using the X; and even those that were literate could not understand the complicated language.   Land was also lost or sold because of the following: non-payment of mortgages and property taxes, fear of ghost if they kept the land, and finally, traumatizing fear of the Ku Klux Klan.

CHAPTER SIX

COURT ACTION TAKEN IN MONROE COUNTY BRING REDEMPTION FOR LAND

SEIZED FROM BLACKS IN THE DOWN-THE-BAY AREA

My brother and I decided on an action plan after living through the experience of seeing our parents and fore-parents land taken, families displaced and then learning about the Statue of Limitation. The action plan was a secret visit to the courthouses in Monroe and Clark Counties to obtain information on regaining our great-grandfather's land. Because these counties are still controlled by Whites, this action had to be inconspicuous. Once the information and records were located we noted there were no microfilm of these records or surveillance cameras in the record room. In other words, if it was discovered what we were seeking and why, the information could easily be deleted and destroyed. During our visits to the courthouses, public information surfaced of land mortgages and how Henry Robinson's land was taken through a land partition sale, which is an unfair but a common practice used to seize land from Blacks and others.

After numerous visits to the courthouses, it was discovered that these old records contained a story of greed, record fraud, trickery, and court battles for land owned by Blacks. Those documents also revealed inferences of fraud and deceit by using and manipulating the Court System for rivalry land. Along with finding those documents,

50

we were fortunate that earlier burnings of courthouses in the South had not extended to Clark and Monroe Counties. The documents showed my great-grandfather owned more than 350+ acres of land in Clark and Monroe Counties. He was also known in the community for owning a farm, animals, money, a juke joint, store and a funeral home. The Whites referred to him as a ``big--*(n--word)*'' so big it was speculated he was killed for that reason.

Before his death, he donated land for a Black school, a church in Claiborne, Alabama, and gave land to family members. Portions of land he did not give away or donate was taken by Eminent Domain and used for part of Highway 84 in Claiborne, Alabama.

Land at this time, was commonly purchased through a Joint Tendency In Common, an agreement where a husband and wife have an equal share and can *sell, deed, will, quitclaim* or transfer land or property to whomever they choose. If one owner dies, the title of the land would transfer to the other living owner(s). Henry's only legal wife, my great-grandmother moved to Mobile, Alabama in 1920. She purportedly signed a quitclaim deed notarized in Mobile, Alabama giving up her rights to the land. However, she could not read nor write and probably had no idea of what she was signing or what would happen to the land. Putting aside what my great- grandmother signed, the law states that the heirs of the last living owner(s) are the ones that will determine what happens to the land. If there are no liens, it may be sold or transferred by the living heirs. If the land is sold, no matter how long the owner has been deceased, and ONE can prove they are legal heirs; that they were not included in the sale or transfer of the land; that they did not receive consideration and they did not transfer rightful interests, then they are entitled to a fair share of the land by law and can legally pursue an interest.

In 1935 Henry and his common-law wife began to mortgage the land, sell acreage, lease and sell timber. There was one White person, a banker and farmer by trade, keeping track of the troubled transactions according to court records because he wanted the land. One of those documents revealed Henry's signature to an affidavit that stated, ``that if the land was ever sold the banker would have first option to buy''. This same land at one time was mortgaged to MJ Robinson, a non-existent person with no birth record. At the top of the document there was a hand written note with initials transferring the property to Henry's daughter, which she deeded to the banker. This deed, however, was proven to be an illegal document.

Henry died under suspicious circumstances in 1955 and a fight ensued for the 300 or more acres of land. The White man who always wanted the land claimed a $600.00 mortgage against the land; the common law wife deeded her part (which she did not own legally) to him, and one of Henry's daughters deeded her part to him for a small amount of money. Henry's remaining children who lived in Chicago, Illinois fought in court to keep the land from the common-law wife and the White man by illustrating and telling of their illegal practices, but it was to no avail. The White man partitioned the land to be sold with an amendment that his wife would obtain a portion because the $600.00 mortgage on the land was also in her name. The land was sold from the Monroe Courthouse steps to the highest bidder (which was the banker) in 1957 for $1,600.00. A $600.00 mortgage was paid to Mr. Deer and the remaining money was divided between Mr. Deer, his wife, the common-law wife and the three siblings. However, this is not the end of the land story.

The White man and his wife had no children, however he did have nieces and nephews. He died in 1976 of cancer and left everything to his wife, who died in 1980. Before her death, she was declared incapable of handling business affairs and was eventually placed in an assisted living home. When she died, her nephew protested the Will, but it was later revealed she was in sound mind when she made the Will. Specifics were made in the <u>Will</u>, but our concern was the property acquired from Henry. We needed to know who held the deeds, because my great aunt—the aunt who was omitted from the original sale in 1957--did not receive her share. This aunt could legally prove she was Henry's daughter because of a birth certificate signed by my great-grandfather, notarized and witnessed by the county clerk. The county clerk was the White man's wife who called for the partitioning of my great-grand father's land.

To date our attorney is facing the nephew's attorney with certified documents used in the land partition sale. This land was purchased by my great-great grandfather and is rich in natural resources, minerals and timber. These court documents are in our possession and are necessary for my aunt to obtain her rightful share. My aunt has quitclaimed the land to her daughter, son, my brother, and me upon final judicial approval. She wanted it known that when she lived in Claiborne, Alabama, her trailer had to be placed on borrowed land because there was ``<u>NO LAND FOR HER AND SHE COULD NOT STAKE A CLAIM--EVEN THOUGH HER DADDY HAD OWNED 350 ACRES OF LAND</u>'' -TODAY, HOWEVER, SHE IS STAKING A CLAIM!!

This brave and courageous lady who left me with so much history now lives in a nursing home; however, she states, ``she is satisfied that some justice was done in trying to recover her father's land''. This case has been assigned a case number and is on file to be settled in the Monroe County Courthouse, Monroeville, Alabama. We are currently waiting for a ruling.

The experience of Blacks after reconstruction was based on injustices, discrimination, prejudices and needs of the majority society to maintain dominance and control. Because of those experiences Blacks have been thrust into a form of psychological slavery wherein some have lost the desire to overcome. This could be the result of a lost sense of family, history, community and closeness with God.

Since integration where communities and a way of life were systemically destroyed, Black history has not been taught on a daily bases and pride seems to be none existence. When pride existed in communities, there was a desire to excel and reach heights simply because family elders said it was possible. Now, where are the family elders and where is the desire to excel by honorable means? It appears that as a race we have moved towards the acquisition of material possessions as opposed to retaining family pride and excelling academically. In this millennium it is imperative to accept and realize we must let go of the mental shackles and regain the zeal needed to overcome racism and discrimination. This was made evident by Senator Trent Lott's statement that this country would have been better if retired Senator Strom Thurman had been President during the 1940's. He merely stated what was in his heart and most probably in the heart of some Americans. These are perilous times and instead of being racist we should be joining to form a better world, to heal past wounds, to ensure that everyone has an opportunity to work regardless to race, creed, color or national origin so that America can truly be the land of the free and home of the brave.

If the aforementioned is to occur, those in charge must let go of the need to control by greed and allow everyone a piece of the American pie. Blacks have been mistreated, maimed, murdered, tricked out of their land, and denied equal access to an education because of testing that is neither cultural free or cultural fair—and in essence are expected to score in a game where they are still in the dugout. Please, consider how is that fair when many community schools for Blacks do not meet the same standards as whites but the testing is the same.

As long as the majority of Blacks remain poor, perform in the lower percentile academically, and have limited access to adequate resources they will not be able to meet criteria established by society. However, for others, education has enabled them to move out of this situation simply because of living in a stable and cohesive environment. Mentoring is another tool to assist those interested in improving academic performance. We must remember W.E.B. DuBois and Booker T. Washington because they stressed that education is the key to opportunity and without it; the door to freedom will remain closed.

For Blacks who were able to obtain an education and employment, limited preparation was obtained to handle the subtitles of racism after integration. Currently, many Blacks, according to Ellis Cose (1993) have been discussing work related experiences as a means of coping with the stress of working in jobs typically held by Whites. In addition, the ``N'' word is not spoken but in some instances the sentiment is present.

In spite of numerous accomplishments since the Civil Rights act of 1964, The United States Equal Employment Opportunity Commission and The Fair Housing Act, inequalities still exist. Discrimination continues to exist even though the concept of integration was to solve this problem. Finally, these laws were passed because of the assistance of Black ministers who during that period were able to matriculate between both worlds.

Coupled with educational problems, racisms, discrimination, the after effect of the Civil Rights Movement, and September 11, 2001, churches are presently demanding improved Christian attitude and race relations. Along with this temperament a State Representative is concerned about a series of news articles printed in 2001 addressing Black land losses across the South and has requested a task force to investigate. This State Representative has also presented a second resolution to the

House Rules Committee for a proposal to investigate other land claims and illegalities.

In summary, numerous young Blacks have not been exposed to the knowledge, wisdom or expertise of the family elder. As a result of this, there is a propensity to take life and family for granted. For some the following motto is applicable: ``It is not what I can do for you, it is what you can do for me'', and ``Why live for tomorrow, it is all about living for today, because tomorrow is not promised''. This type of mindset has resulted in trying to get rich illegally and they have no desire to prioritize future goals or objectives. Another concern is low morals, over exposure to x-rated movies, videos, excessive use of profanity in front of elders, and inappropriate dress. This shift in morality could also include: music with vulgar lyrics, common-law marriages, having children by different men, failure to graduate from high school, Black on Black crime and drug use. This type of behavior must be stopped if we are to save our youth, restore the Black family and rekindle the ``Dream'' of Dr. Martin Luther King.

However, in spite of the issues mentioned, Blacks must also work as a unit to save our children. It is critical to remember that we can accomplish much if we learn how land was stolen, gain financial independence, which was depicted in the community ``Wall Street'' in Tulsa, Okalahoma, establish political involvement for the many and for the few, and finally regain strong religious ties that brought our forefathers through the storms of lynchings, beatings, destruction of communities like Down-The-Bay, and suffering from various degrees of cruelty and humiliation. The question to ponder is ``Where is our sense of community faith today?''

Opportunities to succeed are available but the majority society must allow the playing field to be fair. As long as corporate America is allowed to let jobs go to other countries while Americans are left unemployed, there will be chaos and confusion. Greed seems to be what is leading this country and not the desire to allow everyone an opportunity to excel. With this as a premise, Blacks have been at the bottom of the totem pole and will be pushed further down as long as the rich continue to get richer at the expense of the poor.

If progress is to be ascertained it will have to involve Blacks, Whites, rich, poor and others working together and not against one another. We must remember, we are bound by the common ties of suffering and sacrifices in times of National distress and insecurity, therefore it is unthinkable that we should not be allies in present- and future undertakings. Consequently, nothing can contribute more to the national welfare, regardless to race, than equal justice and opportunity because this is the symbol that represents America to the ``World''. This symbol is representative of those who died for Freedom and Justice for all.

PART THREE

HOME REMEDIES, TABOOS, FOODS, ADAGES, CLEANING METHODS, COUNTER DRUGS, SLANGS AND MUSIC

*TO STOP A TOOTHACHE: PLACE TWO CLOVES BETWEEN THE CHEEK AND THE ACHING TOOTH.

*TO HEAL A BURN: RUB THE AREA WITH ALOE VERA PLANT JUICE, OR SOAK AREA WITH MILK ONCE DAILY FOR FIFTEEN MINUTES.

*TO SOOTHE A BEE STING: USE MEAT TENDERIZER OR RUB TOBACCO ON THE AREA.

*TO HEAL AN OPEN WOUND: CIRCLE THE AREA WITH PETROLEUM JELLY AND SPRINKLE SUGAR—THIS WILL ENHANCE THE HEALING PROCESS AND KILL BACTERIA.

*TO STOP BLEEDING: PLACE SPIDER WEBS ON THE AREA, WHICH WILL CAUSE THE BLOOD TO COAGULATE. (OPEN WOUNDS ONLY)

*FOR FOOD POISONING AND TRAPPED FISH BONES IN THE THROAT: EAT A PIECE OF BREAD.

*WHEN CRITICALLY ILL: PRAYER WARRIORS BAND TOGETHER IN A GROUP TO PRAY FOR HEALING.

*FOR FISH FIN PRICKS: RUB THE SLIME FROM THE FISH ONTO THE AFFECTED AREA—THIS WILL TAKE AWAY THE STING.

*TO TIGHTEN FACIAL MUSCLES: RUB EGG YOLK OVER THE FACE TO TIGHTEN MUSCLES AND ALSO REMOVE WRINKLES.

*FOR NAIL PUNCTURES TO THE BODY: PLACE A PENNY AND A PIECE OF SALT MEAT ON THE WOUND AND WRAP TIGHTLY.

*TO REDUCE HIGH BLOOD PRESSURE: DRINK A SMALL PORTION OF GARLIC WATER AND VINEGAR.

*TO DISSOLVE WARTS: APPLY LEMON JUICE AND CASTOR OIL.

*TO ELIMINATE TAPEWORMS/PINWORMS (COMMON IN CHILDREN 40'S—70'S): INGEST A TEASPOON OF TURPENTINE AND SUGAR, EAT GARLIC, OR RUB KEROSENE AROUND THE NAVEL.

*FOR MUMPS: RUB NECK AREA DAILY WITH SARDINE OIL AND TIE A PIECE OF CLOTH AROUND THE NECK AREA.

*FOR EAR ACHE: USE WARM SWEET OIL ON A COTTON BALL AND PLACE INSIDE THE EAR.

*FOR A CHEST COLD: PLACE FLANNEL CLOTH WITH VICKS OR METHOLATED SALVE ON THE CHEST AT BEDTIME AND WRAP TIGHTLY.

IN THE MORNINGS IT IS IMPORTANT TO WIPE OFF EXCESS--AS OPEN PORES COULD LEAD TO COMPLICATIONS AND/OR PNEUMONIA.

*FOR A SORE THROAT: GARGLE WITH WARM SALT WATER AND DRINK PINEAPPLE JUICE OR PLACE SALT AND PEPPER ON THE PALLID.

*FOR A STUFFY NOSE: SNIFF A SOLUTION OF WARM SALT WATER.

*FOR A FEVER AND COLD: ``STARVE A FEVER, FEED A COLD''. TAKE A DOSAGE OF CASTOR OIL, DRINK PEPPERMINT TEA FROM LEAVES GROWN IN THE BACKYARD OR HOG HOOF TEA MADE FROM HOG TOENAILS, EAT HOMEMADE CHICKEN FEET SOUP, OR DRINK HOMEMADE TODDY (WARM SOLUTION) MADE FROM WHISKEY AND LEMON JUICE.

*FOR A PREGNANCY TEST: TAKE AN ASPIRIN AND IF IT STAYS INGESTED FOR A PERIOD OF TIME YOU ARE NOT PREGNANT. IF IT COMES BACK UP IMMEDIATELY--YOU COULD BE PREGNANT.

*FOR CONSTIPATION: TAKE AN ENEMA WITH WARM SOAPY WATER OR CASTOR OIL.

*FOR HOT FLASHES OR FEELING FAINT: KEEP A HANDERCHIEF SCENTED WITH SPIRIT OF AMONIA HANDY.

*FOR AN ASTHMA ATTACK: PLACE A BROWN PAPER BAG OVER THE HEAD FOLLOWED BY BREATHING IN AND OUT.

*FOR STOMACH CRAMPS: PLACE WARM TOWELS ON THE STOMACH AND DRINK WARM TEA.

*FOR LEG CRAMPS: FOR IMMEDIATE RELIEF DRINK APPLE CIDER VINEGAR.

*FOR YEAST INFECTION AND CLEANLINESS: DOUCHE USING A TABLESPOON OF VINEGAR MIXED WITH WARM WATER.

*FOR DEODORANT: CUT A FRESH POTATOE AND RUB UNDER THE ARM; FOR THE FEET--SOAK IN TEA WATER OR USE BABY POWDER.

*TO REMOVE CALLUS FROM THE FEET: RUB WITH MEAT TALLOW OR PETROLEUM JELLY DAILY.

*TO CLEAN TEETH: BRUSH TEETH WITH BAKING SODA.

*FOR HEATBURN: TABLESPOON OF BAKING SODA IN A 1/2 GLASS OF WARM WATER.

*TO REMOVE SCENT FROM HANDS: RUB HANDS WITH TOOTHPASTE.

*FOR A HANGOVER: DRINK PLENTY OF WATER AND BLACK COFFEE OR PLACE A BAG OF ICE ON THE HEAD.

*FOR A BLACK EYE: PLACE A PIECE OF BEEF STEAK OVER THE EYE.

*FOR BOILS AND KERNELS: RUB WITH TURPENTINE; WHEN BOILS COMES TO A HEAD--SQUEEZE BUT MAKE SURE THE CORE IS REMOVED—THEN USE A SALVE OR PETROLEUM JELLY ON THE AREA. FOR KERNELS: RUB WITH TURPENTINE.

*FOR RINGWORMS: RUB THE AREA RAW WITH A WASH CLOTH THEN PLACE UNRIPEN FIG JUICE ON THE AFFECTED AREA.

*FOR LOW BLOOD PRESSURE: DRINK A SMALL PORTION OF MOGAN DAVIS GRAPE WINE; EAT BEETS OR RARE MEATS.

*FOR A FEVER BLISTER: PLACE EAR WAX ON THE AFFECTED AREA.

*FOR A SWELLING OR FRACTURE: SATURATE WITH WITCH HAZEL DAILY OR SOAK IN BORAX, WARM ALCOHOL, EPSON SALT, OR USE AN ICE PACK ON THE FRACTURE. (HOMEMADE ICE PACK: ICE WRAPPED IN A TOWEL)

*FOR SORE GUMS: PLACE TABLE SALT ON THE AFFECTED AREA.

*FOR HICCUPS: HOLD YOUR BREATH AND COUNT TO TEN FOLLOWED BY DRINKING WATER.

*FOR HEADACHES: APPLY PRESSURE WITH FINGERTIPS PERIODICALLY TO THE TEMPLE ALONG WITH BED REST. APPLT A HEADACHE LEAF AND COLD TOWEL TO THE FORRID.

*FOR ACME: CLEAN FACE DAILY WITH RUBBING ALCOHOL.

*TO REMOVE BLEMISHES: USE COCOA BUTTER, BLACK & WHITE, PONDS, OR ARTA CREAM.

*TO LOWER VITALITY AROUSAL: USE SMALL AMOUNTS OF SALT PETER IN FOOD INTAKE.

*FOR ARTHRITIS: WEAR A COPPER BRACELET ON THE ARM.

*FOR LOCKJAW (FOOT WOUND): CLEAN AND PLACE A COPPER PENNY ON THE WOUND, FOLLOWED BY A SMALL SLICE OF SALT MEAT. WHEN THESE STEPS HAVE BEEN COMPLETED WRAP THE AREA WITH A CLEAN CLOTH.

*FOR DOG DAYS (INFECTION PREVENTION): CERTAIN TIMES OF THE YEAR (SUMMER) WOUNDS ARE SLOW TO HEAL AND EASILY INFECTED. WHEN THIS OCCURS WASH DAILY WITH DIAL SOAP AND USE IODINE.

*TO STOP BLEEDING—COVER THE WOUND WITH PIECES OF BROWN PAPER.

*FOR CALCIUM: INGEST GROUND OYSTER SHELLS MADE INTO A MEAL.

*TO ELIMINATE AN ALCOHOL TASTE OR SMELL: EAT A RAW ONION

*BOTULISM (TOE MAN) FOOD POISON—DRINK MILK

AFTER THOUGHT!

*FOR VITALITY AND ENERGY--EAT RAW EGGS: EYESIGHT--CARROTS: HEALTHY BONES--MILK: LIVER SPLASHES--FISH: PREVENT BLEMISHES AND ACME--EAT SMALL AMOUNTS OF SWEETS: FLUSH KIDNEYS--DRINK PLENTY WATER: AND FOR POTASSIUM--EAT PLENTY BANANAS.

HISTORICAL TABOOS (MOBILE, ALABAMA)

*DO NOT WALK UNDER A LADDER ON FRIDAY THE 13TH BECAUSE IT COULD BRING BAD LUCK.

*IF A BLACK CAT CROSSES YOUR PATH AND YOU DO NOT GO IN THE OPPOSITE DIRECTION IT COULD BRING BAD LUCK.

*IF YOU BREAK A MIRROR YOU COULD HAVE (7) YEARS BAD LUCK.

*DO NOT FISH ON SUNDAY'S BECAUSE IT COULD BRING BAD LUCK AND IT IS NO TELLING WHAT MIGHT BE PULLED FROM THE WATER.

*DO NOT OPEN AN UMRELLA IN THE HOUSE IT COULD BRING BAD LUCK

*THROW SALT OVER YOUR SHOULDER WHEN SOMEONE LEFT YOUR HOME, ESPECIALLY IF YOU DID NOT WANT A RETURN VISIT.

*MAKE A WISH UPON A SHOOTING STAR AND IT COULD COME TRUE.

*DO NOT TELL A BAD DREAM BEFORE THE SUN RISE OR IT WOULD COME TRUE.

*IF YOU CUT YOUR HAIR, FLUSH IT DOWN THE TOILET, BECAUSE IF A BIRD BUILT A NEST FROM IT, IT COULD DRIVE YOU CRAZY.

*IF ONE WAS SASSY TO THEIR PARENTS OR ELDERS, WHEN YOU WENT TO SLEEP--GHOST WOULD NOT LET YOU REST.

*THE FOODS YOU CRAVE WHEN YOU ARE PREGNANT WOULD BECOME THE BIRTHMARK OF THE BABY.

*WHEN YOU'RE PREGNANT, DO NOT POKE FUN AT ANYONE OR THE BABY COULD BE MARKED AND HAVE FEATURES LIKE THAT PERSON.

*WHEN PREGNANT AND SUFFERING WITH HEARTBURN, THE CAUSE WAS BELIEVED TO BE THE BABY HAD A HEAD FULL OF HAIR.

*A BABY BORN WITH A VEIL OVER ITS EYES COULD SEE GHOSTS, FEEL THE PRESENCE OF SPIRITS AND SEE THE FUTURE.

* THE 7TH CHILD BORN IN A FAMILY WAS BELIEVED TO HAVE GOOD LUCK AND THE ABILITY TO HEAL.

*IF YOU TELL LIES, LIE BUMPS WOULD APPEAR ON THE TONGUE AND CAUSE PAIN.

*TO STOP DOGS FROM DEFECATING, PULL YOUR PINKY FINGERS IN THE OPPOSITE DIRECTION.

*IF IT RAINS AND THE SUN CONTINUES TO SHINE, PUT A NAIL
THROUGH A TIN CUP AND PLACE IT ON THE GROUND AND YOU COULD
HEAR THE DEVIL BEATING HIS WIFE.

*IF IT RAINS ON A DAY A PERSON IS BURIED, THEY WOULD GO TO
HEAVEN.

*IF YOU CAN FIND THE END OF THE RAINBOW, THERE WAS A POT OF
GOLD.

*DO NOT LEAVE A HAT YOU HAVE WORN AT SOMEONE'S HOME BECAUSE
THEY COULD DO EVIL THINGS BY USING THE HAT BAND.

*YOU CAN TELL WHEN A PERSON WAS ABOUT TO DIE BY A RATTLING
SOUND IN THE THROAT--COMMONLY CALLED THE DEATH RATTLE.

*BY LOOKING AT THE TIP OF A NEWBORN'S EAR, YOU COULD TELL
WHAT THE SKIN TEXTURE WAS GOING TO BE.

*OLDER PERSONS COULD TELL IF YOU WERE PREGNANT BY THE DOUBLE
BEAT THEY SAW IN YOUR THROAT. THEY COULD ALSO TELL THE
BABY'S SEX BY THE SHAPE OF THE WOMAN'S STOMACH.

*KEEP YOUR HEAD COVERED TO PREVENT CATCHING A COMMON COLD
DURING INCLEMENT WEATHER. IT WAS BELIEVED BY FAMILY ELDERS
THAT THE VIRUS WOULD ENTER THE BODY THROUGH THE TOP OF THE
HEAD.

*YOU COULD ALWAYS TELL WHEN BAD WEATHER WAS COMING BECAUSE
ANIMALS WOULD BUNCH TOGETHER.

*IF YOU CARRIED A RABBIT'S FOOT, CROSSED YOUR FINGERS, OR
FOUND A FOUR LEAF CLOVER IN A FIELD OF THREE LEAF CLOVERS IT
COULD BRING GOOD LUCK.

*IF A PERSON WERE MURDERED, A TREE WOULD GROW ON THE BURIAL
SPOT, WHICH SIGNIFIED INNOCENCE.

*IF THE FOG WAS MISTING ACCORDING TO THE ELDERS, IT WAS A
SIGN OF RAIN AND IF IT WAS NOT, IT WAS GOING TO TURN COLD.

*ALL DREAMS HAVE A MEANING, EXPECIALLY FISH DREAMS. A FISH
DREAM IMPLIED THAT SOMEONE IN THE FAMILY WAS PREGNANT.

*DEATH IN THE NEIGHBORHOOD USUALLY CAME IN THREES.

*WHEN A PERSON WAS GOING TO DIE, DEATH WOULD USUALLY APPEAR
THREE TIMES IN THEIR DREAMS.

*A HOWLING DOG MEANT SOMEONE IN THE NEIGHBORHOOD WAS GOING TO DIE.

*FULL MOON USUALLY MEANT TEMPERS WOULD RISE WHICH USUALLY LEAD TO VIOLENCE. FOR OTHERS THE FULL MOON WAS AN INDICATION OF A GREAT TIME TO GO FISHING.

*EAT OYSTERS ONLY IN THE MONTHS THAT HAVE AN `R' OTHERWISE THE OYSTERS WOULD BE MILKY AND HAVE LITTLE TASTE.

POPULAR FOODS FROM THE PAST   (MOBILE, ALABAMA)

BREADS

BISCUITS
HOECAKES
HOTWATER CORN BREAD
CRACKLIN BREAD/MUFFINS
BUTTER MILK CORNBREAD
YEAST ROLLS
DUMPLING

MEATS AND VEGETABLES

*PIG FEET & PIG EARS
*CHITTERLINGS, TRIPE & HOG MAWS
*ALL EATABLE SEAFOODS W/COLE SLAW
*COLLARD GREENS & HAM HOCKS
*RAW OYSTERS/CRACKERS & HOT SAUCE
*OKRA FRIED WITH ONIONS & BACON
*CREAM CORN/FRIED CORN/ FRIED TOMATOES
*FISH FLAKES/JACK MACKERAL/ONIONS/POTATOES/EGGS
*CHICKEN FEET & RICE
*COOKED CABBAGE W/POTATOES & WHOLE OKRA
*FRIED RABBIT/SQUIRREL W/GRAVY
*DEER SAUSAGE/ OR DEER ROAST & GRAVY
*OKRA W/PEAS, SNAP OR BUTTER BEANS
*FRIED SQUASH & CUCUMBERS/VINEGAR
*BARBECUE GOAT/PICKLED PIG FEET/HEAD CHEESE/SOUSE
*BAKED OPOSSUM & BAKED SWEET POTATOES
*BUTTERMILK & CORNBREAD W/DRIED BEANS AND SAUSAGE
*KALE/TURNIP GREENS & DUMPLING/FRIED COLLARDS & EGGS
*BAKED CHICKEN/TURKEY W/STUFFED CORN BREAD DRESSING
*SMOTHERED CHICKEN/BARBECUE RIBS/MEATLOAF/HAM
*MOUNTAIN OYSTERS—COW TONGUE—KIDNEYS
*SMOTHERED BEEF OR PORK LIVER & ONION
*FRIED TOMATOES/SLICED TOMATOES & MAYONNAISE
*POTATOES: MASHED/BOILED/BAKED/FRIED OR PONES
*MUSH/GOULASH/GUMBOS/OF OKRA-CHICKEN-VEGETABLE-SEAFOOD
*SUCCOTASH
*FLAPJACKS/SYRUP/FAT BACK/--OATMEAL/WHEAT/HOMINY
*SOUPS: VEGETABLE, CHICKEN, TURKEY, BEEF, OR OXTAIL
*BRISK STEW MEAT COOKED W/POTATOES, TOMATOES & GRAVY
*CHICKEN & DUMPLINGS OR STEWED CHICKEN & RICE
*CABBAGE/TURNIP GREENS W/ GREEN ONIONS & PEPPER SAUCE
*PIG TAILS W/ DRIED BEANS OR PEAS
*SMOTHERED POTATOES, ONIONS AND SAUSAGE
*CHEESE GRITS/GRITS W/FRIED FISH, OYSTERS, OR SHRIMPS
*GREEN ONIONS/ BOILED/FRIED EGGS W/CHEESE
*RICE SAUTEED W/BUTTER; ROUND STEAK W/RED EYE GRAVY
*PORK & BEANS W/WEINERS
*SOUTHERN FRIED CHICKEN/LIVERS/GIZZARDS OR BAKED ROAST
*CHEESE IN MACARONI OR POTATOE CASSEROLE

SWEETS

HOMEMADE ICE CREAM
GINGER & SHORTBREAD
TEA CAKES/FUDGE
LEMON/BLACKBERRY PIE
RICE/EGG CUSTARD
ANGEL/JELLY CAKE
WATERMELON/JELLO

DRINKS

LEMONADE/KOOL AID
EGG NOG
WHISKEY TODDY
COFFEE & CREAM
SWEET WATER/TEA
COCOA

THE INTERPRETTIVE ANALYSIS OF THE MEANING OF SOUL AND SOUL FOOD

SOUL: IS A SPECIFIC WORD USED AND REFERRED TO BY BLACKS DENOTING IDEAS, THOUGHTS, FEELINGS, EMOTIONS, AND BODY RHYTHM IN ACCORD WITH TASTE FOR CLOTHES, MUSIC, FOODS AND ONE'S BEING.

SOUL FOODS: THE NAME GIVEN TO SPECIFIC FOODS THAT WERE GENERALLY COOKED OR PREPARED BY BLACKS USING MEATS, ANIMAL INNARDS, ALL PARTS OF THE PIG, SEAFOODS, ROOTS, OR VEGETABLES, DICED WITH SPICY SEASONING AND COOKED IN GREASE, LARD, OR OIL. DURING THE TIME OF SLAVERY, ANIMAL INNARDS, EARS, TONGUES, HEADS, NECKS, FEET AND TAILS WERE THE DISCARDS OF WHITES AND WERE CONSUMED BY BLACKS. THEY ALSO GREW VEGETABLES, FISHED, AND HUNTED. EXTRAS SUCH AS: FLOUR, CORN MEAL, AND SUGAR WERE GIVEN TO BLACKS BY THEIR MASTERS TO PREPARE MEALS. BLACKS PREPARED FOOD OVER AN INDOOR POKER STOVE OR IN A BLACK BOILING POT OVER AN OUTDOORS FIRE. IN OTHER WORDS, THE WAY THE FOOD WAS PREPARED, HOW IT WAS PREPARED, AND WHAT WAS PREPARED BROUGHT ABOUT THE NAME AND THE REFERENCE MEANING OF SOUL FOOD. FINALLY, SOUL FOOD IMPLIED THAT ALL MEALS WERE PREPARED IN LOVE AND FROM THE MIND, HEART AND SOUL.

A QUOTE FROM MY GRANDMOTHER REGARDING THE PREPARATION OF FOOD WAS: ``THE FOOD MIGHT NOT BE HEALTHY TO EAT, BUT ITS GOOD EATING, YOU'LL HAVE A FULL BELLY, AND ITS NOURISHMENT FOR THE SOUL''.

THE MEANING OF HAVING THE BLUES & THE BLUES MUSIC FROM THE BLACK PRESPECTIVE

HAVING THE BLUES: A SAYING USED OFTEN BY BLACKS DENOTING A FEELING OF DESPAIR. IT IS ALSO HAVING A DOWN AND OUT FEELING CAUSED BY MANY THINGS SUCH AS: NO MONEY, LOVE AND FAMILY PROBLEMS, SICKNESS, DEATH OF A FRIEND OR FAMILY MEMBER, AND PROBLEMS WITH THE CHILDREN.

THE BLUES MUSIC: THE FATHER OF THE BLUES IS WILLIAM CHRISTOPHER (W.C.)HANDY WHO PLAYED A CORNET. HE PLAYED ``FLATBED THIRDS AND SEVENTHS'' TO WHAT IS CALLED THE BLUES. HE DIED ON MARCH 28, 1958 IN NEW YORK. THIS MUSIC IS ABOUT INNERMOST FEELINGS OF DESPAIR EXPRESSED THROUGH VOICE PROJECTION AND LYRICS ABOUT LIFE AND LIVING. BLUES IS ALSO PLAYED TO A RHYTHM BEAT THAT WAS MORE THAN LIKELY, NOT WRITTEN. MUSICIANS DID NOT HAVE TO HAVE KNOWLEDGE OR SCHOOLING BUT RATHER IT WAS SIMPLY A FEELING, A BEAT, AND A WAY OF EXPRESSION PUT TO MUSIC. WHEN THE EXPRESSION WAS PUT TO MUSIC OTHERS COULD JOIN-IN BY EITHER DANCING, PLAYING A HORN, PIANO, DRUMS, HARMONICA, WHISTLE, STOMP THEIR FEET, OR CLAPPING THEIR HANDS.

THESE FEELINGS OF THE BLUES WERE EXPRESSIONS OF LIFE'S PROBLEMS AND DIFFICULTIES. THIS MUSIC WAS A WAY FOR BLACKS TO FEEL FREE DURING THE 40'S, 50'S, 60'S, & 70'S, TO EASE STRESS AND COPE WITH PERSONAL PROBLEMS AND RACISM. THE JUKE BANDS AND SINGERS PROJECTED THEIR VOICES WITH MOANS, HOLLERING, PLEADING, SNORTING, CRYING, AND GROANING TO ALLOW AUDIENCES AN OPPORTUNITY TO EXPLODE AND FEEL A SENSE OF FREEDOM. WITH THESE SONGS AND LISTENING TO THE MUSIC THERE WAS NO SHAME IN EXPRESSING THEIR FEELINGS. IT WAS ALL RIGHT TO EXPRESS THESE FEELINGS BECAUSE EVERYBODY KNEW WHAT THEY WERE SINGING ABOUT. IN SUMMARY, ALL BLACKS HAD EXPERIENCED THE BLUES, COULD INDENTIFY WITH AND BE A PART OF THE FEELING OF THE SONGS AND THE MUSIC.

◄ *W.C. Handy*

BLUES QUOTE: " I HAVE HAD MY FUN YA'LL, EVEN IF I DON'T GET WELL NO MORE"

JUKE JOINT: A PLACE COMMONLY CALLED A HOME FOR THE BLUES

70a

*YOU MUST WANT TO BE SOMEBODY IN ORDER TO BE SOMEBODY

*DO NOT BURN BRIDGES YOU MIGHT HAVE TO COME BACK ACROSS

*CANTCHE DONTCHE HAIR: CAN'T COME IT AND DON'T YOU TRY

*BEBE DEE HAIR: HARD TO COMB HAIR/KNOTTY

*AUNT HAGGERTY CHILDREN: REAL NAUGHTY CHILDREN

*RAISING CAIN: DISAGREEMENT/AUGUMENTATIVE

*DO NOT MAKE SOME GLAD TO SEE YOU TWICE: GLAD TO SEE YOU COME BUT MUCH HAPPIER TO SEE YOU GO

*EGG ON YOU FACE: BEEN SHAMED

*IF YOU LIE DOWN WITH DOGS——YOU GET UP WITH FLEAS

*IF YOU MAKE YOU BED HARD——YOU HAVE TO LIE IN IT

*PREGANCY: ONE NIGHT OF PLEASURE——NINE MONTHS OF PAIN

*BETWEEN A ROCK AND A HARD STONE

*CAN NOT SEE THE FOREST FOR THE TREES

*GOT THE CARA MARGUS AND THE SHOOT THE SHOOTS: DIARRHEA

*IF YOU CAN NOT KEEP A SECRET——WHAT MAKES YOU THINK I CAN

*A HARD HEAD MAKES A SOFT BEHIND

*A WHISTLING WOMAN AND A CROWING HEN COMES TO NO GOOD END

*A BIRD IN THE HAND IS WORTH TWO IN THE BUSH

*A FOOL AND HIS MONEY ARE SOON PARTED——HERE TODAY——GONE TOMORROW

*BE LIKE THE WISE OWL: THE MORE HE HEARD THE LESS HE SPOKE—— THE LESS HE SPOKE THE MORE HE HEARD

*IF TONGUE AND TEETH CAN NOT GET ALONG SOMETIMES- WHAT DO YOU EXPECT FROM YOUR FELLOW MAN

*THAT RED THING IN YOUR MOUTH (TONGUE) WILL SAY ANYTHING YOU WANT IT TO SAY AND YOU ARE RESPONSIBLE FOR IT

*THERE IS NO PLACE LIKE HOME- YOU CAN GO THERE WHEN YOU CAN GO NO PLACE ELSE

*GOD BLESS THE CHILD THAT HAS HIS OWN

*EARTH IS NOT YOUR HOME- YOU ARE JUST PASSING THROUGH- SO LEAVE FOOTPRINTS FOR OTHERS TO FOLLOW

*DO NOT COUNT YOUR CHICKENS BEFORE THEY HATCH

*IF YOU DO NOT KNOW WHERE YOU ARE GOING YOU WILL NEVER GET THERE

*THE FIRST PERSON YOU MEET WHERE YOU ARE GOING——IS YOURSELF

*TIME WAITS ON NO ONE-BUT EVERYONE WAITS ON TIME

*A GOOD RUN IS BETTER THAN A BAD STAND

*I RATHER BE A LIVE CHICKEN THAN A DEAD DUCK

*WALK CAREFUL AMONG THE DEAD AND TRUST NOT A LIVING SOUL

*YOU ARE ONCE A MAN OR WOMAN BUT TWICE A CHILD

*IGNORANCE OF THE LAW IS NO EXCUSE——IF YOU DO THE CRIME—— THEN DO THE TIME

*FOR ANY ONE BETWEEN THE AGES OF 14-20- YOU ARE MORE THAN A BOY OR GIRL——BUT NOT YET A MAN OR A WOMAN

*KNOW YOUR PLACE AND STAY IN IT

*STILL WET BEHIND THE EARS——THE SMELL OF BABY'S MILK IS STILL ON YOUR BREATH

*JUST AS SURE AS THE SUN SHINE——IT WILL ALSO RAIN

*THE DARKEST HOUR IS JUST BEFORE THE DAWN

*YOU GOT HERE AS QUICK AS YOU COULD- BUT I GOT HERE SOONER—— BECAUSE I DOTTED THE (I) AND CROSSED THE (T) IN TRICK

*YOU ARE SLICK——BUT YOU CAN STILL STAND TO BE GREASED

*IF YOU CAN NOT STAND THE HEAT——STAY OUT OF THE KITCHEN

*SOME PEOPLE CAN STEAL THE SWEETNESS OUT OF GINGER BREAD

*YOU CAN LIE BEFORE QUICK CAN GET READY

*I AM GOING TO WHIP YOU TIL YOU ROPE LIKE OKRA

*REMEMBER YOU CAN NOT STAND STILL—YOU CAN NOT GO BACKWARDS-
YOU MUST MOVE FORWARD

*TODAY IS THE TOMORROW YOU DREAM ABOUT

*TODAY'S YOUNG IS TOMORROW'S OLD

*TIME IS OF THE ESSENCE

*BEHIND EVERY DARK CLOUD THERE IS A SILVER LINING

*LET GO AND LET GOD

*I AM GONNA MAKE YOU CLIMB A GREASY WALL

*WIN LIKE YOU NEVER WON BEFORE—LOSE LIKE YOU LIKE IT

*DO NOT LOSE YOUR FOCUS—KEEP YOUR EYE ON THE PRIZE

*DO NOT PUT OFF UNTIL TOMORROW WHAT YOU CAN DO TODAY

*SPARE THE ROD AND SPOIL THE CHILD

*WHAT GOES ON IN THE DARK WILL SURFACE TO THE LIGHT

*YOUR WORD IS YOUR BOND

*IF YOU LIE YOU WILL STEAL

*BETTER LATE THAN NEVER

*ONLY THE STRONG WILL SURVIVE

*THE BEST THINGS IN LIFE ARE FREE

*SMILE AND THE WORLD SMILES WITH YOU—CRY AND YOU CRY ALONE

*A FAMILY THAT PRAYS TOGETHER STAYS TOGETHER

*THE TRUTH WILL SET YOU FREE

*BLOOD IS THICKER THAN WATER

*LIFE IS WHAT YOU MAKE IT

*NOTHING BEATS A FAILURE BUT A TRY

*YOU DO NOT MISS YOUR WATER—UNTIL YOUR WELL RUNS DRY

*WHAT GOES AROUND COMES AROUND

*ALL CLOSE EYES AIN'T SLEEP--ALL GOODYBYES' AIN'T GONE

*ITS' BETTER TO GIVE THAN TO RECEIVE

*WHAT GOES UP MUST COME DOWN

*LOVE IS AS LOVE DOES

*BEAUTY IS ONLY SKIN DEEP AND UGLY IS TO THE BONE

*NOTHING FROM NOTHING LEAVES NOTHING

*BLACKER THE BERRY SWEETER THE JUICE
 AN OUNCE OF BLACK BLOOD IN A WHITE PERSON——MADE THEM BLACK

*WHAT YOU ARE GOING TO BE——YOU ARE NOW BECOMING

*IF YOU DON'T ASK——THE ANSWER IS ALWAYS NO——BUT IF YOU ASK——
THE ANSWER MAY BECOME YES, NO, OR MAYBE SO

*FOR EVERY PROBLEM THERE IS A SOLUTION——AND FOR EVERY
SOLUTION——THERE WAS A PROBLEM

*MONEY IS THE ROOT OF ALL EVIL

*CHANGE MONEY——DO NOT LET MONEY CHANGE YOU

*PRETTY IS AS PRETTY DOES

*STICKS AND STONES MAY BREAK MY BONES——BUT WORDS WILL NOT
HURT ME

*I AM BLACK AND I AM PROUD

*BUZZARD LUCK: CAN'T KILL NOTHING- AND WON'T NOTHING DIE

*FOOT LOOSE AND FANCY FREE

*YOU CAN BE LONELY BUT NEVER ALONE

*MIND OVER MATTER: I DON'T MIND AND IT DON'T MATTER

*OUTTA SIGHT AND OUTTA MIND

*UP THE CREEK WITHOUT A PADDLE

*GOOD RIDDANCE TO BAD RUBBAGE

*ONE MAN'S TRASH IS ANOTHER MAN'S TREASURE

*I CAN FORGIVE BUT NOT FORGET——LIVE AND LET LIVE

*MY WAY OR THE HIGHWAY

*DON'T KNOW YOU'RE POOR UNTIL YOU GET MORE

*A LEAF DO NOT FALL FAR FROM THE TREE

*ONE BAD APPLE SPOILS THE WHOLE BARREL

*A ROLLING STONE GATHERS NO MOSS

*AN EMPTY WAGON MAKES A LOT OF NOISE

*I WOULD RATHER BE AN OLD MAN DARLING THAN A YOUNG MAN'S
 FOOL

*AN OUNCE OF PREVENTION IS WORTH A POUND OF CURE

*IF I HAD YOUR HAND--I WOULD TURN MINE IN

*HOME IS WHERE THE HEART IS

*DON'T BUY YOUR LOVER NEW SHOES, THEY MIGHT USE THEM TO WALK
 ON YOU

*DAMN IT TO HELL--CAUSE THE FUN IS ALL OVER

*SELF PRESERVATION IS THE FIRST LAW OF NATURE

*COME HELL OR HIGH WATER

*ITS' ALL OVER BUT THE SHOUTING

*I'M IN BLUE HEAVEN

*DON'T KNOCK IT IF YOU HAVEN'T TRIED IT

*I FINALLY SEE DAYLIGHT

*THAT PUT A HURT ON ME

*SHUCKING AND JIVING

*MOMMA `N NEM WANT YOU

*CRUMB SNATCHERS

*PLAYING THE FIELD

*BEING EATEN OUT OF HOUSE AND HOME

*ALL I CAN DO IS SMOKE AND BURN

*COUGH IT UP AND TELL IT LIKE IT IS

DURING THE TURN OF THE CENTURY, SOUTHERN BLACKS SPOKE WITH A DISTINCT FLAT ACCENT AND WHITES SPOKE WITH A DRAWL. MANY STILL DO TODAY, AND ITS' CALLED A SOUTHERN ACCENT. FEW OBTAINED SCHOOLING DURING THIS TIME, THEREFORE THEY DID NOT KNOW WHERE TO PLACE EMPHASIS ON CERTAIN LETTERS USED TO FORM WORDS, AND SOME COULD NOT READ OR WRITE. DUE TO THIS FACT, WHATEVER LANGUAGE THEY HEARD OUTSIDE OR LEARNED IN THE HOME WAS WHAT THEY PRECEIVED AS CORRECT ENGLISH. FOR EXAMPLE, FROM ONE OF THE OLD ADAGES "CANTCHE DONTCHE HAIR: IS SPELLED EXACTLY AS PRONOUNCED AND THE IMPLICATION IS "CAN'T COMB IT, DON'T YOU TRY".

PIG LATIN: A LANGUAGE DIALECT USED LOCALLY BY BLACKS TO COMMUNICATE. THIS LANGUAGE WAS NEVER WRITTEN DOWN BUT USED FREQUENTLY AND SPOKE FLUENTLY. EXAMPLE: WHAT YOU SAY (WAS PRONOUNCED AND SPOKEN AS) UT WAY OOWAY AY SAY.

CLEANING AND RESTORATION METHODS: (MOBILE, ALABAMA)

---

*HOT TAR TO STOP LEAKS ON ROOFS AND-INSIDE DRAINS

*MIXTURE OF FLOUR & WATER OR CREAM OF TARTAR FOR PASTE OR STARCH

*LEMON JUICE TO REMOVE STAINS ON CLOTHES OR RUST SPOTS

*TO REMOVE MILDEW/FUNGUS/MOLE, PRESSURE WASH HOUSES, STAINS IN GLASSES OR COUNTER TOPS USE A COMBINATION OF WATER AND PUREX

*APPLY OIL OR PEANUT BUTTER TO REMOVE STICKY LABELS

*TO CLEAN THE BOTTOM OF A STAINED IRON OR POT RUB IN BLACK DIRT

*TO SHARPEN A KNIFE USE A FILE OR CEMENT ROCK

*USE OYSTER SHELLS FOR A DRIVEWAY OR WALKWAY

*TO POLISH AND RESTORE GLOSS TO FURNITURE AND MAINTAIN LONGEVITY USE LINSEED OIL

*TO CLEAN LEATHER AND SOME LIGHT SPOTS USE HAIR SPRAY

*TOOTHPASTE OR BAKING SODA: CLEANS SILVER—AND REMOVE STRONG ODORS OR SMELL FROM THE HANDS

*CREOSOTE: DEODORIZER AND KILLS MANGE ON DOGS

*DEVIL LYE: MAKE SOAP—UNSTOP DRAINS AND TOILETS

*GREASE STAINS ON SILK: SPRINKLE WHITE POWDER ON THE AREA

*CLEAN LAMP SHADES: APPLY WHITE CORN MEAL AND THEN BRUSH

*STORED CLOTHING: APPLY MOTHBALLS FOR FRESHNESS

*SHOE SHOP: SHINE/RESTORE SHOES—REPAIR PURSES—BELTS

*CLEAN JEWELRY: USE A FLANNEL CLOTH

*REPAIR TORN OR HOLES IN CLOTHES: APPLY CLOTH PATCHES
REMOVE GUM FROM CLOTHES: RUB ICE OVER THE GUM UNTIL IT HARDEN--THEN LIFT

*OLD STOCKINGS: PLACE OVER HAIRBRUSH—THEN BRUSH TO REMOVE LINT FROM CLOTHES

---

*DIRTY CAR OIL: APPLY TO THE SOIL TO KILL WEEDS

*TURPENTINE: THIN PAINT

*GASOLINE: REMOVE PAINT STAINS—HAND CLEANER

*CLOTHES & SHOE DYES: RESTORE COLOR; CHANGE FABRIC COLORS

*WHISK BROOM: USED TO SWEEP OUT HARD TO GET PLACES—REMOVE LINT FROM CLOTHES

---

*PAREGORIC: SETTLE THE STOMACH OF BABIES & ADULTS

*DEWEES: FEW DROPS IN MILK WILL HELP BABY SLEEP

*SCOTT'S EMULSION: SETTLE AN UPSET STOMACH

*COD LIVER OIL: CLEAR UP SPOTS IN THE FACE

*COCOA BUTTER: A BLEACH FOR DARK SPOTS ON THE SKIN

*PONDS VANISHING CREAM/NOXZEMA: SKIN CLEANER FOR THE FACE

*SPIRIT OF AMMONIA: SNIFF WHEN A PERSON FAINT OR FEELS FAINT

*THREE (666'S): MEDICATION FOR HEAD COLDS

*HEAT: AN ARTHRITIS OINTMENT FOR SORE JOINTS

*HORSE LINIMENT: AN ARTHRITIS OINTMENT FOR SORE JOINTS

*CAMPHO PHENIQUE: LINIMENT OINTMENT FOR SORE JOINTS

*MENTHOLATUM: CHEST OINTMENT FOR HEAD COLDS & CONGESTION

*VICKS SALVE: CHEST OINTMENT FOR HEAD COLDS & CONGESTION

*CASTOR OIL: HEAD COLDS AND CONGESTION

*GOODY POWDER/COKE: HEADACHES

*ST. JOSEPH/BAYER ASPIRIN: HEADACHES

*VICKS COUGH DROPS: IRRITATED THROATS AND COLDS

*TURPENTINE & SUGAR: TAKEN INTERNAL FOR COLDS/WORMS

*PHILLIP MILK OF MAGNESIUM/BLACK DRAUGH: LAXATIVE

*VINEGAR/ALUM: DOUCHE SOLUTION FOR WOMEN

*SALT PETER: USED TO LOWER SEXUAL DRIVE

*BLUE MAGIC OINTMENT: BODY CRABS & LICE

*WITCH HAZEL/BORAX: SWELLING AND ABRASIONS

*EPSON SALT: BODY SOAK FOR RELIEF OF SORENESS AND SWELLING

*TINCTURE MERTHIOLATE: ANTISEPTIC MEDICATION

---

*TURPENTINE: ANTISEPTIC MEDICATION

*IODINE/MERCUROCHROME: ANTISEPTIC MEDICATION

*PEROXIDE/BORIC ACID: MIXTURES USED TO CLEAN WOUNDS

*PETROLEUM JELLY: ANTISEPTIC MEDICATION AND SKIN SOFTNER

*JOHNSON BABY POWDER: SMELLY ODORS AND DIAPER RASH

*SWEET OIL: EAR ACHE

*PALM OIL: SMOOTHER SKIN

*MINERAL OIL: CLEAN THE SCALP

*SULPHUR AID & GLOVERS MANGE MIX: MISTURE USED TO GROW HAIR

*EYE WASH: SOLUTION FOR THE PINK EYE DISEASE

*LISTERINE: MOUTH WASH

*BEES WAX: BODY WARTS

*MUM/SECRET: DEODORANT

*CALAMINE LOTION: POISON IVY/SKIN IRRITATIONS

*GLYCERINE: HAIR SOFTNER

*GERITOL: LIQUID VITAMIN FOR ENERGY

*DR. TICHENOR'S ANTISEPTIC: A LIQUID TAKEN INTERNALLY FOR CONSUMPTION, PILES, AND ANYTHING ELSE THAT WAS WRONG WITH YOU

YESTER YEARS: SLANG WORDS AND PHRASES OF THE BLACK COMMUNITY

*KNOBS & KICKS: SHOES
*THE FUZZ/THE MAN/PIGS: POLICE
*PUT YOUR EYES ON: GLASSES
*SPORTY/FLASHY DRESSER: LOUD CLOTHES & JEWELRY
*FINE: NICE BODY SHAPE
*WHAT'S HAPPENING: A POPULAR PERSON
*GRUB/GREASE: EAT
*A PIG/GUSHY: FAT
*HARD HEADED: DO NOT FOLLOW DIRECTIONS
*DOUGH/GREEN: MONEY
*PIMP/SQUEAL: TELL WHAT ONE KNOWS
*SHARP AS A TACK: DRESSED WELL
*STEPPING HIGH: EVERYTHING GOING FOR YOU
*RUN IT BY ME: TELL ME ABOUT IT
*A BRAIN: A SMART PERSON
*KNOCK SENSE: COMMON SENSE
*OKIE DOKIE: EVERYTHING IS ALL RIGHT
*SQUARE: NERD
*SLICK: CON ARTIST
*HEN/BROAD: LADY   CHICK: GIRL
*TONGUE TIED/CAT GOT YOUR TONGUE: NOT TALKING
*JIVE TALKER/SHOOTING THE BREEZE/MACKER: A FLIRTING MALE
*WHEELS/RIDE: A CAR
*SUGAR COAT: COVER UP
*FLICK: MOVIE
*PUT THE MOVE ON/MACKING: MAKE A PASS
*PLAYING GAMES: NOT FOR REAL
*NEED HELP: SOMETHING NOT APPEALING TO THE EYES
*FULL OF CRAP: PLAYS TOO MUCH/NOT SERIOUS
*YOUR FLAVOR: BOY OR GIRL FRIEND
*KITCHN IS STINKING: FOOD SMELLS GOOD
*OUT ON THE TOWN: GOING OUT FOR A GOOD TIME
*WHIPPER SNAPPER: YOUNG—FAST LIVING PERSON
*UNCLE TOM/RAT: TELL EVERYTHING TO THE WHITE MAN
*TATTLE TELLER/SING LIKE A BIRD: ONE THAT TELLS EVERYTHING
*ROPE LIKE OKRA: KNOT UP
*CUTTING UP: SHOWING OUT
*FOOL/CRAZY: CARRY ON FOOLISHNESS
*OLD COON: OLD PERSON, TRYING TO ACT YOUNG
*DOING BAD: DOWN AND OUT ON YOUR LUCK
*FRESH: MAKING OUT OF THE WAY REMARKS
*DRINK LIKE A FISH: DRINK TOO MUCH
*LIVER LIVERED/ CHICKEN/TURKEY: SCARED
*COTTON PICKING HANDS OFF ME: INSULT/MOVE YOUR HANDS
*HUM BUG/SCRAP: FIGHT
*CONTRAPTION: SOMETHING MADE THAT COULD GET YOU KILLED
*MEDDLING/DIPPING: ATTENDING TO SOMEONE ELSE'S BUSINESS
*PLAY THE DUZ/JINK: TALK DEGRADING ABOUT SOMEONE
*BREAD BASKET: STOMACH
*SCOLDING: CHASTIZING
*SUGAR COAT: COVER UP

*SHUCKING AND JIVING: PLAYING
*CUT OUT: LEAVE OR TO GO
*DIRT CHEAP: BARGAIN
*NUTS/LOOSE SCREW: CRAZY, LOST OF MEMORY
*HARD BOIL: WILL NOT CHANGE VIEWS EASILY
*RAT/SPILL THE BEANS: REVEAL, TELL
*KNOCKED UP: PREGNANT
*CHICKEN HEAD/DUST ON A JUG/BE BE DEE: SHORT HAIR
*PUTTING ON: PRETENDING
*CHEWING THE FAT: TALKING WITH NO SUBSTANCE
*GIFT OF GAB: GREAT TALKER
*BAD NEWS: WARNING TO STAY AWAY FROM SOMEONE
*BLACK SHEEP: WITHDRAWN FROM THE FAMILY
*SAD: NO GET UP AND GO ABOUT ONESELF
*PAINTED HUSSY: LADY OF THE EVENING
*SNEAKY PETE: DO THINGS AND DO NOT CONFESS TO THEM
*GAS ON YOUR CHEST: WANT TO GO FOR A RIDE
*SENT PACKING: TOLD TO LEAVE
*STACKED: A FINE SHAPED BODY OR 36-24-36
*SQEAKY CLEAN/NO FLIES: REAL CLEAN
*SILVER SPOON: BORN TO HAVE GOOD LUCK AND MONEY
*LIQUID SUNSHINE: RAIN
*GOOD RIDDANCE: TO LEAVE—GO
*NOSE PROBLEMS: NOSY OR IN OTHER PEOPLE'S BUSINESS
*STUCK UP/MISS ANN: WANT TO BE CUTE
*TURNING OVER A NEW LEAF: NEW BEGINNING
*FOOT LOOSE AND FANCY FREE: NO ATTACHMENTS
*ICE CUBE/ICEBERG: REAL COLD/NO FEELINGS
*COMB YOUR KITCHEN: HAIR ON THE NAPE OF THE NECK
*SLUMMING: GOING TO JUKE JOINTS/STAYING OUT LATE
*LIVING LARGE/BIG TIME SPENDER: LIVE EXPENSIVELY
*COO COO/BANANAS: GONE CRAZY
*CRUISING FOR A BRUISING: A BEATING/LICKING
*YOU DIG: DO YOU UNDERSTAND
*RAINING CATS AND DOGS: DOWN POUR OF RAIN
*EAGLE EYES: SEE EVERYTHING
*GUTS: STAMINA
*FRIED, DYED, LAID TO THE SIDE: CONK/HAIRDO FOR A MAN
*JAIL BIRD: BEEN INCARCERATED
*CRIB/PAD: HOUSE
*MAIN SQUEEZE: STEADY GIRL OR BOY FRIEND
*CRASH: GO TO SLEEP
*WHAT'S UP: WHAT GOING ON
*HEIFER: WOMAN WITH A NASTY ATTITUDE
*MUSHY/LOVEY DOVEY: VERY LOVING
*LEFT A BAD TASTE: DO NOT TRUST
*GOODY, GOODY TWO SHOES: A PERSON THAT DOES NO WRONG
*SCHOOL HOUSE SCOTCH/SHORTY OUT THE JAIL HOUSE: WINE
*CRABBY: FUSSY
*CRIPPLE CRAB: ALWAYS TRYING TO PULL SOMEONE ELSE DOWN
*SNAKE: BACK STABBER
*SWEET PERSON: NICE PERSONALITY

*TWO BITS: A QUARTER
*FILLING OR GAS STATION: SERVICE STATION
*ON THE RAG: LADIES MONTHLY PERIOD
*WOMANLISH/SMELLING YOURSELF/BESIDE YOURSELF: SASSY
*THE CRUMBS: LEFTOVERS
*GO FLY A KITE: GO AWAY
*NOT WHAT YOU ARE CRACKED UP TO BE: NOT WHAT YOU REALLY ARE
*HALFERS: HALF OF WHAT YOU GOT
*SAVE ME THE SHORT: CIGARETTE BUTT
*WOLF: BRAZEN/HARSH
*GREAT BEYOND: DIED
*GROWING LIKE A WEED: BODY MATURING FAST
*HIT BELOW THE BELT: TALKING BAD ABOUT SOMEONE
*IT IS ABOVE MY HEAD: DO NOT KNOW WHAT THE TALK IS ABOUT
*PULL THE STRING: FLUSH THE TOILET
*A DOG: LOW DOWN PERSON
*GIMME SOME ROOM: NEED SOME SPACE
*MAKING OUT: ROMANCING
*MR. KNOW IT ALL: ONE WHO THINKS HE KNOWS EVERYTHING
*ASHY: NEED A BODY LOTION
*EGGING ON: PUSHING UP A DISTURBANCE
*EGGS ON YOUR FACE: SHAMED
*RIPE FOR THE PICKING: A YOUNG LADY IN PUBERTY
*FEZ UP: TELL THE TRUTH
*PEACHES AND CREAM: GET ALONG WELL/SMOOTH
*IN THE FAST LANE/SMOKING/HOT TO TROT/FAST AS A WHIP/
*FIRE CRACKER: LIVING AHEAD OF THE TIMES
*BOY YOU ARE GOING TO GET A KILLING: BEATING
*BIG TIMER/LIVING LARGE/BIG HEAD: SPENDING LOTS OF MONEY
*JUMPING JACK: CANNOT KEEP STILL
*NEAT AS A PIN: NEAT AND CLEAN
*I'M GOING TO TAR AND FEATHER YOU: TIE UP AND BURN
*DEATH RIDING YOU: A PERSON LIVING LIFE CARELESSLY
*PEANUTS: LITTLE OR NO COUNT
*BLOWED UP: TAKEN OUT OF PROPORTION
*NO BACKBONE: NO SPUNK
*THE DOGS ARE BARKING: FEET ARE HURTING
*BUCKETS OF WATER POPPING OFF: SWEATING
*NO WAY: IT DID NOT HAPPEN LIKE YOU SAID
*HOLIER THAN THOU: LOTS OF HOLES IN YOUR CLOTHES
*FINE RAGS: NICE CLOTHES
*FROM UNDER THE SPOTLIGHT: NOT BEING WATCHED
*YOU SHUCKING ME/PULLING MY LEG: YOU FOOLING ME
*NIP IT IN THE BUD: STOP IT BEFORE IT STARTS
*SHUT EYE: SLEEP
*SEWED UP/LIPS SEALED/COVERED: GOT EVERYTHING TOGETHER
*A LITTLE BOOGER: SMALL TOTTLER
*SEE YOU LATER ALLIGATOR AFTER WHILE CROCODILE: GOOD BYE
*CHOO CHOO: THE TRAIN
*BEEN BURNED: GOT A SEXUAL TRANSMITTED DISEASE
*CUT BUDDIES: FRIENDS YOU HANGOUT WITH

*COOL BREEZE: NEATLY DRESSED PERSON
*YOUNG STUD/BUCK: YOUNG FELLOW
*BLOOD/CUZ: A RELATIVE
*QUIETNESS KEPT: DO NOT TALK
*LONG/CONE HEAD: HEAD WAS NOT SHAPED IMMEDIATELY AFTER BIRTH
*MY FLAVOR/MY THING: BOY OR GIRL FRIEND
*REEFER/MARYJANE: MARIJUANNA
*UG MO: REAL UGLY PERSON
*RED DEVIL/SPEED: A DRUG USED FOR AN UPPER/HYPED
*HICKEY: A PASSION MARK
*RIDING THE WHITE HORSE/ON THE NEEDLE: HEROIN/ADDICT
*WINE-O: A DRUNK
*JOY JINKING: MAKE INSULTING REMARKS

TOAST OF OLD: THROUGH THE LIPS--OVER THE TONGUE--AROUND THE GUMS—LOOK OUT STOMACH—HERE I COME

TOAST OF OLD: HERE'S TO IT—TO DO IT—WHEN YOU GET TO IT; IF YOU DON'T DO IT—WHEN YOU GET TO IT—YOU WANT GET TO IT -TO DO IT

SLANG WORDS (CONSIDERED INSULTING) USED BY BLACKS IN REFERENCE TO WHITES: whitey, flat butts, pale face, pinkies, hoosiers, hunkies, hicks, swamp rats, poor white trash, white pork, soda crackers, oreo, miss bitch, half pints (men), blue eyed devil, snake, red necks, hillbillies, vanilla wafers, cajun, nigger lover (if associates with Blacks), and mousie

SLANG WORDS (CONSIDERED INSULTING) USED BY WHITES IN REFERENCE TO BLACKS: nasty coloured folks, uncle tom, smoky, shine, nigger, porch monkies, boy (grown man), black sambo, bitches, bastards, liver lips, big butts, sticky fingers, horse mouth, cuck-a-bug, topsy, alligator bait, sonny boy, gal, stud, aunt jamima, pick ninnies (children), coon, George (porters), hyena, big foot, darkie, bucky beaver, stink pots, heathens, and buck wheat

YESTER YEARS SLANG WORDS AND PHRASES OF THE BLACK COMMUNITY WERE WORDS AND PHRASES USED BY BLACKS' DURING THE 1940'S—1970'S AND PASSED DOWN THROUGH THE YEARS.   THESE SLANG WORDS AND PHRASES WAS A MEANS FOR BLACKS' TO COMMUNICATE, BY PLACING EMPHASIS ON CERTAIN WORDS THAT DENOTED MEANING AND EXPRESSION. THESE SLANG WORDS AND PHRASES WERE NOT WRITTEN BUT WERE USED DAILY IN REFERENCE TO ANIMALS TO DENOTED TEMPERAMENT, LOOKS AND

ACTIONS. FOR EXAMPLES: FAT AS A PIG—OVER WEIGHT, BULL HEADED—STUBBORN, AND CHICKEN—COWARD— ARE A FEW OF THE SLANG EXPRESSION USED BY BLACKS DURING THAT OF PERIOD OF TIME.

DURING THAT TIME PERIOD FAMILY ELDERS WERE ALSO KNOWN TO USE DOGS, PIGS, COWS, EAGLES, AND OTHER ANIMALS TO DESCRIBE THE WIND, WEATHER, THE SENSES, AND BODY PARTS. THIS WAS DONE AS THEIR METHOD OF COMMUNICATION AS MANY COULD NOT READ OR WRITE. THIS ORAL HISTORY ADD FURTHER CREDENCE TO THE USE OF SLANG WORDS. IN OTHER WORDS BLACKS FORMULATED THEIR OWN LANGUAGE AND USAGE.

BLACK MUSIC

BALL ROOM MUSIC: PROGRESSIVE/MODERN JAZZ, A SOUND THAT HAD AN AIR OF SOPHISTICATION BECAUSE ONE HAD TO HAVE KNOWLEDGE OF MUSICAL INSTRUMENTS, MUSICAL SCALES AND HARMONIZING. THIS MUSIC WAS PLAYED AND DANCED TO AT SOCIETY FUNCTIONS.

BE BOP: A FORM OF JAZZ PLAYED IN THE 1940'S—50'S; THIS TYPE OF MUSIC IS PLAYED WITH A FAST TEMPO AND SMALL ENSEMBLE. THIS MUSIC WAS A FAVORITE OF AND DANCED TO BY TEENS AND YOUNG ADULTS.

BLUES: REFER TO THE 'BLUES' IN PART THREE OF THIS BOOK..

CALYPSO: MUSIC FROM TRINIDAD THAT WAS POPULAR IN THE 50'S.

CANE MUSIC: SOUNDS FROM PIPES MADE FROM CANES AND HARMONIZED WITH DRUMS—POPULAR IN THE 40'S AND 50'S.

DOO WOP: MUSIC THAT WAS POPULAR IN THE 50'S & 60'S AND SANG IN A COMBINATION OF CROONING AND IMITATED SOUNDS TO FORM DIFFERENT PITCHES AND CHORDS BASED ON THE SEVEN DEGREES OF THE SCALE—THEN COMING TOGETHER IN THE SAME RHYTHM.

GOSPEL HYMN: BASIC CHORAL MUSIC SANG IN THE AFRICAN AMERICAN CHURCHES. THIS MUSIC WAS DERIVED FROM SLAVES AND SANG WHILE THEY WORKED IN THE FIELDS. IT IS OFTEN HUMMED IN SOLO AND IN GROUPS—IT IS SANG WITH MUSIC OR ACAPULCO. ONE REASON FOR SINGING IN THE FIELDS WAS FOR THEM TO COMMUNICATE; AND THE REASON FOR THE HUMMING WAS SO THE DEVIL COULD NOT UNDERSTAND WHAT THEY WERE THINKING AND PRAYING ABOUT.

HONKY TONK/GUT BUCKET: NAME GIVEN TO MUSIC PLAYED IN JUNK JOINTS AND DIVES. THIS MUSIC WAS PLAYED WITH AN ENSEMBLE OF DRUMS, HORNS, HARMONICA, GUITAR, RUB BOARDS, TAMBOURINES, PIANO AND/OR SINGER(S). THE HONKY TONK IS VERY SIMILAR TO THE BLUES.

HYMNS: CHORAL CHURCH SONGS.

JAM SESSION: MUSIC PLAYED BY TWO OR MORE PLAYERS COMING TOGETHER TO IMPROVISE AND TUNE UP.

JAZZ : BLACKS CREATED THIS MUSIC FROM A COMBINATION OF RAGTIME AND BLUES SOUNDS; WHEN PLAYED, IMPROVISION AND DELIBERATE DISTORTION OF PITCH, VOICE, AND MUSICAL SOUNDS ARE USED. THE JAZZ MUSIC IS OF A RHYTHMATIC BEAT THAT ORGINATED FROM AN UNKNOWN ORIGIN ABOUT 1917. EARLY BLACKS LISTENED TO THIS PARTICULAR TYPE OF MUSIC BECAUSE OF ITS' EFFECTS ON MOOD, THE FEELING OF OBLIVION, AND THE ONENESS FELT WHILE LISTENING TO THE BEAT AND SOUND. THOSE JAM SESSIONS WERE USUALLY HELD IN DIMLY LIT PLACES WITH A RELAXED SETTING—ALCOHOL WOULD BE AVAILABLE, AND OF COURSE THERE WOULD BE DANCING !

QUARTET: ENSEMBLE OF FOUR SINGERS—ACCOMPANIED BY STRING INSTRUMENTS.

PSYCHEDELIC/FUNK ROCK: LOUD MUSIC USING THE SYNCHRONIZING OF ELECTRIC GUITARS AND ROTATING PSYCHEDELIC LIGHTS. THIS FORM OF MUSIC WAS ORIGINATED AND POPULARIZED BY JIMI HENDRIX IN THE 60'S.

REGGAE: JAMAICAN MUSIC VERY POPULAR IN THE 70'S.

RAGTIME: PROGRESSION OF HARMONY —THE PIANO WAS THE PRIMARY INSTRUMENT.

ROCK AND ROLL: IS A MUSIC OF BLACK ORIGIN BUT WAS IMITATED AND PROFITED FROM BY WHITES. SOME ORIGINAL BLACK ROCK AND ROLLERS' ARE AS FOLLOWS: LITTLE RICHARD, FATS DOMINO, CHUCK BERRY AND BO DIDDLEY. THIS MUSIC WAS POPULAR IN THE 50'S AND 60'S; ADDITIONALLY, ANOTHER ORIGINAL WAS CHUCK WILLIS, WHO WROTE "I DON'T WANNA HANG UP MY ROCK AND ROLL SHOES CAUSE ROCK AND ROLL IS HERE TO STAY". THIS WAS RECORDED AND SANG BEFORE THE RISE OF ELVIS PRESLEY.

RHYTHM AND BLUES/POP: SOUNDS OF THE 1950'S WITH THE LIKENESS OF BLUES BUT REFLECTED JOYFUL AND HAPPY TIMES. IT IS IDENTIFIED WITH BLACKS BECAUSE IT WAS ORIGINATED AND ROOTED IN BLACK CULTURE. ARTISTS: ROSCO GORDON, ROBERT JOHNSON & ROBERT BELFOUR.

SCAT SINGING: A STYLE OF JAZZ SINGING WITH NONSENSE SYLLABLES, WHICH WAS POPULARIZED BY CAB CALLOWAY IN THE 1920'S.

SWING: A FORM OF BIG BAND JAZZ POPULAR IN THE 30', 40'S, AND 50'S & 60'S. THE DANCE CALLED THE SWING WAS ORIGINATED FROM THIS MUSIC IN THE 50'S AND IS STILL POPULAR TODAY.

MOBILE BLACKS

he Mobile Review

BILE'S FIRST AND BEST MAGAZINE

December–January 1947

25c Per Copy

— No. 3

Unpainted "shotgun" houses were a familiar sight.

SHOT GUN HOUSES (A VIEW FROM FRONT STRAIGHT TO THE BACK)
WERE BUILT IN THIS MANNER FOR VENTILATION—DOORS WERE
OFTEN LEFT OPEN IN THE SUMMER FOR VENTILATION BECAUSE OF
THE HEAT AND HUMIDITY.

PART FOUR: MOBILE BLACKS ON REVIEW 40'S, 50'S, 60'S & 70'S

- SOCIETY MEETINGS

- SOCIAL FUNCTIONS

- PERSONALITIES

- LOCAL TALENT/CREOLES

- HAIR STYLES AND FASHIONS

ALABAMA STATE DENTAL ASSOCIATION HOLDS MEET IN MOBILE

Tobin, prominent Mobile
leads the organization.

Dentists who attended the Mobile Convention this year. This
photograph was taken at the Utopia, Inc. Club House on pic-
turesque Mon Luis Island

CHARTER MEMBERS OF THE ALABAMA STATE DENTAL ASSOCIATION WHO MET IN
SELMA, ALABAMA IN 1946 TO FORM THE ORGANIZATION

ALTHURISTIC BRIDGE CLUB HOLDS FIRST ANNUAL BALL

own above are the Althuristic Bridge Club
rs taken at their first annual ball given at the
Home on Thursday night, November 13, 1947.
s and members of the Althuristic Bridge Club
s. Rena Hill, President; Miss Frances Washam,
resident; Miss Beulah Green, Recording Sec-
: Mrs. Evana Jackson, Financial Secretary; Mrs.
Jones, Treasurer.; Mrs. Mary E. Hall, Statis-
Mrs. Thelma Glenn, Chaplain; Mrs. Ruth Hen-
, Reporter; Mrs. Geraldine Finch, Business
ger; Mrs. Daisy Barnett, Mrs. Dorothy Bracy,

Mrs. Cora Walker and Mrs. Elizabeth Cooke. Mrs.
Cooke, one of the active members in the club, was
taken ill before the dance, and died shortly afterwards.

Decorations were beautiful and appropriate. The
stage was covered with the canvas of a bronze-sleepy
girl against a background of clouds. One side of the
stage was drawn a shapely sleeping sepia beauty.
Many delightful souvenirs were given away. Shown
below is a cross section of the crowd that attended
the affair and had a merry time.

TAN MYSTIC CLUB'S FIRST ANNUAL BALL SPARKLING AFFAIR

PERSONALITY PAGE

. and Mrs. W. L. Russell pose in front of their auto-
le soaking in the warm rays of the autumn sun. Dr.
Mrs. Russell nee Lyndall Borras are active civically
socially. Dr. Russel is president of the Colored Carni-
ssociation. Mrs. Russell is well known for her pleasing
nality and smart attire.

Mrs. Bessie Abrams, one of Mobile's oldest and most popular beauticians, pauses in front of her home
for this snapshot. She is the mother
of the editor of The Mobile Review.
Mrs. Abrams, better known as "Pat"
to her host of friends, resides at 452
Congress Street.

s. William Blanchard Marshall, better known
her friends as the admirable "Sherry." She is
rming, smart attractive person, easy to know
ike. The Marshalls reside at 1053 Davis Ave-
Mr. Blanchard is a member of the Merchant
ies.

Miss O. L. Hill, one of Mobile's first graduate registered
nurses, and midwife, is well loved by Mobilians and especially her "children" who are constantly praising her
goodness. Always ready to lend a helping hand, wherever
and whenever the need arises, Miss Hill is one of those
few persons who is unfailingly unselfish. May she prosper.

STAND'
UP
COMEDIAN

1967
Jackie ('mons') Mabley

JORDAN WAS IN TOWN

At a recent date, the Colored Carnival Association brought to Mobile Louis Jordan, whose scintilating rhythms set toes to tapping. The orchestra played at the Davis Avenue Recreation Center, where throngs listened and swayed to the renditions that have made him famous.

Sidney Wright, Peggy, throaty vocalist with the Jordan Orchestra, and Vernon Z. Crawford, Circulation Manager for The Mobile Review, watch the gay goings-on.

THE TALENTED HOWARDS

rs. Howard cheerfully serves one of her patrons in her lovely new shop.
rs. Howard's charming personality has endeared her to her patrons.

Vivacious Dorothy shown outside one of the academic buildings at Wilberforce University which she attends. Dot will soon be home for the Christmas holidays.

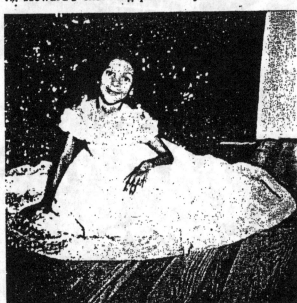

le Gwendolyn Howard in a pretty pose. Pert
endolyn can play the piano skillfully as well as
: charming.

MEET A TALENTED FAMILY

rs. Ida Yotes Howard has the things that many

lovely children, a lovely home and a satisfying career.

Mrs. Ida Yates Howard began her work as a beautician working as an operator in the shop of Mrs. Gussie Hendricks at 401 N. Ann Street. As Mrs. Hendricks became unable to do the work Mrs. Howard became manager. In 1928, being farsighted in her business prospects, she moved her shop to Glennon Avenue. At this time she was the only operator. Today Mrs. Howard is located at 1302 Davis Avenue where she maintains a thoroughly eqiupped shop with a skilled efficient staff of courteous operators. She does a volume of business and has for years been one of Mobile's leading beauticians.

Mrs. Howard has two lovely daughters, Dorothy and Gwendolyn. Dorothy, is a senior at Wilberforce University, Wilberforce, Ohio. She will graduate in June of 1948. Lovely Dorothy is attractive and vivacious and enjoys increasing popularity in Mobile's social circle.

Mrs. Howard's younger daughter, Gwendolyn is an accomplished pianist. She began playing at a tender age. showing promise of becoming a excellent pianist, Gwendol a is well known throughout the city for her musical

Remmeber when those lovely lasses were famous and on their way to stardom. Yes, during the nineteen thirties they were really going to town. New York, Chicago, Buffalo and other cities of the North. Starting out in a big way at The Pelican Roof in gay old New Orleans "The Pope Sisters," four girls with a

combination of "The Mills Brothers" and "The Boswell Sisters" musical talent and ability turned out to be a real national find and from the start they were a sensation. Starring at the Lafayette Theater in New York they literally stormed the country and thrilled huge audience after audience with their scintillating beauty and melodic voices. And did they receive ovations?—I should saaa-y so.

The first most striking thing about them was their striking beauty and the second was the apparent joy which they derived from their acts. Some of their numbers which they became famous in rendering were: "Why Do You Make Me So Glad," composed by Miss Odile. 'It Don't Mean a Thing," and "Underneath the Harlem Moon," "I Can't Give You Anything But Love," "Minnie the Moocher's Wedding Day" and "That Sentimental Man from Georgia." Their most famous encorses were: "Yeah Man, O Yeah Man." and "Say It Isn't So."

They broadcast regularly over WODX. Battle House, Mobile; Saenger Theater, Pensacola, Fla.

This is what The Pittsburg Courier had to say— "Pope Sisters" (Dixie's Hot Spot of Radio.)

The charming Creole beauties, the Pope Sisters will soon invade the North on their first tour of the country .They are the radio sensations of the Southland, and the most popular entertainers in Mobile, Alabama. Their gifted talent, combined with their fascinating beauty, caused them to be declared the marvel of the profession . . . These young ladies are full-blooded Creoles and have never been but a short distance from their home town . . . their sparkling personality and pleasing manner is remarkable . . . Their youthfuld attractiveness has already earned them high praise and appreciation by not only everybody who knows them, but thousands of wealthy white people all over the Southland. The recent discovery of the fascinating quartet has been hailed with requests coming from all sections by theatrical producers and promoters seeking their services.

At the Lafayette Theater 7th Avenue and 131st Street, their Harlem Moon Dream was realized.

There they made a debut among the most famous and most glamorous of any team in the history of the vaudevillians. They had many chances to star in motion pictures but they in such demand in person on the stage that they never realized that ambition to its fullest degree.

Three of these beauties are still holding their own in the world of beauty in young matronhood and

Y. M. C. A. FASHION CONTEST COLORFUL, CLOSE AND EXCITING

Mrs. Clayton McCord

Villie Mae Calvin. First ner. representing Calvin's ss Calvin wore a stunning al gown of net with jet sequins adorning the fash- plum. Her accessories of e highlighted by a wild purplish hues (not pictur- in the gown revealed high er. slippers. each adorned tstone which correspond- tiny circlet worn around o accentuate the sweet- -line.

Grill, located on 8 Gov- reet, is one of the popu- nts in the city. Calvin's , is located at 552 Davis he Grills are noted for

Runner-up. Miss Carter looked charming in an unusual color-com- bination . . . cerise and ivy green. The dress boasted a voluminous skirt with the interest centered on a back bustle gracefully draped.

With the new ivy green bustle- back dress, Miss Carter wore cerise gloves and bag. On her hair. she wore a black net mantilla-like head covering spangled with sequins of ivy green and cerise.

Miss Carter represented Jim's Old Fashioned Barbecue, 858 Davis Ave- nue. Jim's Old Fashioned Barbecue

who desire fine foods and the best in barbecue.

Co-first Prize Winner represent- ing Leonard's Dress Shop. Mrs. Mc- Cord wore a black street outfit with black accessories touched with nail- heads. Over her arms she wore a six skin scarf of Kolinsky furs.

The dress becoming in length was draped to one side and girded with satin. A black and gold encrusted broach and gold ear-rings complet- ed the outfit. Msr .McCord's black suede pumps as well as the dress emphasized the new closed-in look. The wide black framed her face

Read what Miss Hattie Besteda, one of Mobile's foremost authorities on Style and Beauty has to say about the new trend in these fields

r the December.- Janu-
issue of the Mobile Re-
we interviewed Mrs.
tie Besteda, on of this
on's foremost authori-
on Style and Beauty, for
s concerning the new
d and how to achieve the
w Look." Mrs. Besteda
out some very practical
of information to be
by women from 16 to
See if you agree. Here
some simple rules that
gives for good groom-
and style:

Wear a fashion-wise
ure. The drastic change.
othes calls for a neater,
e feminine look as sym-
ed in the coiffure "The
Look" created by Mrs.
eda. This is especially
for holiday parties.

Be alert to news ideas
smetics. Let your beau-
n try some of the newer
es of powder and lip-
on you.

Be kind to your nails.
e your nails manicured
larly. Select a shade
wears well and use
hing lipstick.

Keep face, throat in
make-up tone. Be sure
your throat color mat-
your face, especially

"The New Look' Coiffure
By Mrs. Hattie Besteda

when you wear a low cut gown as shown on the model.

5. Have fun with false hair, providing you don't overdo it. Pin-on pieces may be obtained from your beauty parlor and matched per_fectly with your hair. Never use so much that it will immediately detected.

6. Eat for good health and good looks such things as you know are good for you, fruit, cheese, eggs, meat green salads, milk and rye bread. Too much soda pop and sweets will make you blemish and put on pounds where you don't want to.

7. Shampoo your hair frequently. It's an outmoded theory that washing your hair too frequently will harm it. With the new shampoos, washing it becomes almost a treatment. These products help rid your hair of dandruff and leave it nice and soft.

8. Try new fashions with a new look. Miss Esther

Evans models a black afternoon dress, the new long
length with a cascade of daz-
zling sequins forming a glit-
tery yoke in the dress and
falling in double folds to the
waist.. With this dress she
wears smart black suede
shoes, matching suede bag
and velour hat of the same
color touched with ostrich
plumes. Miss Evans' ear-
rings contain the same daz-
zling color compination of
the sequins in her dress. Her
stockings are the new dark
shade, her fingertips and lipstick match, and she uses a
velvety brown tone of powder — all for the New Look.

9. Have a facial and body massage. Treat yourself to these thoroughly relaxing sessions at your beauty parlor.

10. Always be dainty and feminine. Femity and quiet, serene calm are the keynotes to the new trend.

Miss Esther Evans, Style Conscious and well-dressed wears an afternoon
...fit

Rear View of "The New Look"
Created by Mrs. Besteda

PART FIVE: SCHOOLS, TEAMS, CURRICULUM AND STUDENTS

*SCHOOL PICTURES (40'S. 50'S, 60'S & 70'S) OF

*HEART OF MARY

*DUNBAR

*CENTRAL HIGH

*MOBILE COUNTY TRAINING

*MOBILE ASSOCIATION FOR RETARDS

MOBILE REVIEW

HEART OF MARY HIGH SCHOOL FOOTBALL SQUAD
STILL UNDEFEATED CHAMPIONS

A photograph of the Heart of Many High School Football Team taken on the campus

Top photo- Miss Heart Of Mary and her escorts, including the Pep squad, members, of the football team at coronation game. Bottom: Scene on Davis Avenue...

'~p photo-- Heart Of Mary's band on parade. Bottom-- Beautiful float with iss Heart of Mary and court in the parade.

HONOR STUDENTS AT DUNBAR HIGH SCHOOL

The above students are honor pupils for the first quarter at The Dunbar High School. The teachers and parents are proud of the fact that they have chosen the path of study instead of the path of laziness and "The Live Wire" is offering a cash prize for any student in the above school who makes the honor roll for two consecutive quarters during this term. Reading left to right: Edna Mae Autry of 535 Live Oak St., the daughter of Mr. and Mrs. John Autrey; Robert Clayton, Jr., age 13, the son of Mr. and Mrs. Robert Clayton, Sr., of 1105 State St., a member of the Mathematics and Geography Club and secretary of Dunbar's Teen Ager's Club; Silvia F. Watson, age 13, the daughter of Mr. and Mrs. John Watson of 403 N. Lafayette St. She is a freshman and the vice president of The American Junior Red Cross of Mobile County, secretary of Y-Teens of Dunbar and has been chosen by the faculty of Dunbar to represent the school on a visit to the Freedom Train. Almeda Tunstall age 13, the daughter of Mr. and Mrs. Willie Tunstall of 1333 Congress St.

Left:- Charming young mother and her Tid-bits.
Mrs Olivia mae Wiley of "Texas Hill" poses for us with Little Audrey Mae, Michael Conrad and Clifton Levi. Mrs. Wiley is a Member of the Warren Street Methodist Church and Young Adult Methodist Fellowship and prominent in several social clubs of the Gulf City. Full of wit, humor and business is Mrs. Wiley.

Dr. B. F. Baker, former principal of the Mobile County Training School, is Director of this credible institution, located on St. Anthony Street. Central High has an enrollment of approximately 800 students.

Dr. B. F. Baker, principal of Central High and Director of Negro Education in Mobile County, takes ime out from his multitude of duties to pose for the ditor of The Mobile Review.

Miss Dora Lee Williams, attractive young Mobilian, acts as vice principal at Central High School. She attracts with her sparkling personality.

The Mobile Review is All Right with us.

Lovely Central Lassies . . . . .

Here's looking at you!

Little Miss Janie Baker, daughter of Dr. Baker smiles shyly at the camera.

An apple for the editor.

Hundred dollar smiles and they mean it!

CENTRALIANS KEEP VERY BUSY

Mr. _____, serious minded young president of the Twenty-one Club.

vn above left to right are Miss Aline Edwards, Secretary to Dr.
r; Miss Edna Thomas, instructor of business at Central; and un-
ified instructor working in the office where all matters are dis-
d of silently and efficiently.

. T. McClain, one of the few qalified librarians
city checks the dates on a book, while her as-
. Miss Rose Moore, cheerfully answers a ques-
y one of the students. Mrs. McClain's efficiency
l known throughout the city.

Miss Virginia Blunt, instructs an English class. Miss
Blunt is noted for her ability to get things done and is
very active civically and socially.

p of students study earnestly and quietly in

A portion of the members of the Twenty-one Club,

WILDCATS OF CENTRAL HIGH

The football season is over for the Wildcats of Central High and all athletic interest is turned toward basketball. Basketballs are flying every where as both girls and boys are sharpening their eyes for the present cage season with an eye on the city and conference diadems. With the above happenings on the Central campus it is only fitting and proper to say a few last words for the first Central football team, which won the conference championship and shared city championship with Heart of Mary. The Wildcats were under the tutelage of Head Coach Alphonse A. Gordon and his able assistants, Lemuel K. Keeby, Virgil J. Rhodes, and H. Clinton Sunday. These men welded together a team of warriors that were hard to defeat, a feat attested by their record which showed only one regular season defeat against the best competition offered by Alabama and the Gulf Coast. The Marion Wildcats were undefeated in conference and city competition and lost their only regular season game to the powerful Thundering Herd of Parker High in Birmingham, a team which has not lost a game in the last five years and unscored on in the past two seasons until they met the maroon clad men of Coach Gordon.

The Central Huskies closed this years campaign with a loss to the Lions of Booker T. Washington High in the Third Annual Youth Bowl Classic held in Xavier Stadium December 13. The bid to play in the Youth Bowl came after the Wildcats defeat of the Mobile Training School Whippets Thanksgiving Day. The Central stalwarts used a wide open type of offense and the stadium being a quagmire the fleet Wildcat backs were never able to get going for any substantial gains and ball handling was almost impossible. The breaks decided the game and it so hap-

Continued on page   31

Frances Marie Clauselle
Beautiful Little Senior of Central High School.   She is proud of her school and her Principal.
Frances is the daughter of Mrs. Sadie W. Evans

Top Photo– New Mobile High   School ("Central High")
Below–   Huge crowd enjoying a football game. (Pick out Wilmer
G.)

MISS COUNTY AND ATTENDANTS

To be elected "Miss County" is a signal honor long to be cherished by any "Countian". "Miss County" for 1947 is Miss Lucile Hicks of Senior 1 class sponsored by Mrs. Yvonne King. The honor entails that the recipient is a good citizen of the school, possessed of a good character, studious and respected by both faculty and student body.

It is relevant that Miss Hicks is representative of her section of the Senior class; they stand high in everything concerning the welfare of County High. She exemplifies the County tradition of high ethical character. She is an earnest student and a fine young lady who believes in service and believes in seeking nobler goals.

On "Home Coming," Miss County sat resplendent in her box attended by two other young ladies, Miss Dorothy Patterson of Senior 2 class, sponsored by Mr. Henry C. Turner; and Miss Rosetta Everette of Junior 1 class, sponsored by Mrs. Gladys O. Gordon.

Miss Patterson (right) is among the most active County students. Among her duties are president of the Ki-Yi Club, and attendance deputy. Miss Everette (left) is among the most lady-like students of the school and is very active in school life. She is the President of District 2 of the N. H. A. Club and second vice president of the State N. H. A. Club.

Miss Everette journeyed to Langston, Oklahoma, last July to attend the National N. H. A. Conference in an official capacity. In addition to these important offices she is also vice president of the Maximus Club, and "A Big Sister."

ALPHA DELTA SIGMA SCIENCE CLUB

Alpha Delta Sigma Science Club of Mobile Training School joins the junior chapter of Alabama Association of Science Teachers. The club was awarded a certificate for the presentation of an exhibit at the Science meet December 5-6, 1947.

The members of Alpha Delta Sigma Science Club are engaged in investigations in the field of Cl...

Herbert Beverly, a senior member recently completed a successful experiment of Electrolysis of water.

The members of Alpha Delta Sigma Science Club give a salute to James Williams, Herbert Beverly, Dorothy Floyd, Deloris Johnson, and Val...

One of the nations' greatest coaches spoke the truth when he put into words what so many of us well know.

"The transition from childhood to adulthood is a period of rapid and revolutionary development involving a considerable amount of physical, mental and emotional strain.

New interest, new companions and new activities present a constantly shifting series of challenges. Although only a small percentage of adolescents become so mentally ill as to require hospitalization, the majority of normal high school boys and girls develop many emotional problems that call for sympathetic understanding and guidance.

Unfortunately many high school students have the wrong conception of what is involved in growing up. In their eagerness to assume the privileges and responsibilities of adulthood, too many succumb to adult vice and strain-producing activities which, in time, lead to social maladjustment.

At the Mobile Training School, we try to aid in teaching students what is socially right in providing opportunities to practice these knowledges through our Physical Education and Athletic Program.

We start the term with football. No boy in the school is turned down if he is willing to stick to the training rules. This year we developed a large number of freshman which made up most of the team. This group of youngsters in conference competition won two, tied two and lost two games. They are not discouraged at all with this record.

They understood very well they were playing for the first time against players in their fourth year of football. With this record they will be the team to beat next year.

We are well pleased for in this activity we were able to teach them how to grow up.

Basketball is next on our program with a large number in on every practice both boys and girls. We have their interest and the rest will be easy.

After basketball, we follow that up with softball and track.

In the past two years we have had some intramural boxing which we plan to continue. To our surprise when we first introduced boxing some few years ago both the boys and girls reported for the sport. We were at a loss for what to suggest to the girls when one of the coaches came up with the suggestion "Let them take part" and that we did. I am sure they will be back this year with as much interest as before.

It is through these activities that those of us in the Athletic Department try to do our best in helping the school provide opportunities to teach the student what is socially right by practice of the knowledge learned on the playing field.

CURRICULUM

MATHEMATICS DEPARTMENT

Mathematics at the Mobile Training School i signed to meet the needs of the students in daily As its purpose or aim, the department recognize following:

1. Accuracy and skill in the fundamental esses.

2. Specific knowledge useful in life.

3. Knowledge and power to apply mathema concepts.

4. Guidance and further exploration of the of mathematics.

At the various levels or grades, students are opportunity to elect one phase of mathematics v will in turn lead to the next course in sequenc present, the school offers Business Mathem (Arithmetic); First Year Algebra; Second Year bra; and Plane Geometry. In the not too distanc ture, Solid Geometry will also be offered.

THE 1947 EDITION OF THE WHIPPETS   OF MOBILE COUNTY HIGH SCHOOL

Reading from left to right, back row; Mr. Chas.Rhodes, assistant coach; Mr. Roscoe Gailliard, head coach; Clifford Saunders, Earl Wilson, Otis Andrews,Jessie Smith, Wash Taylor, Coleman Davis, Miss V. Deloris Johnson, H. C. Thomas, Ceasar Hope, Cleo-ford Daniels, Curleë Pate, Benjamin July, W. T. Daniels, Isiah Franklin, Mr. Willie Oscar Gailliard, as-sistant coach; Professor J. T. Gaines.

Front row, left to right: Isiah House, Z. Simpson,Celestyne Jackson, Walter Page, Jack Brown, James Fletcher, E. W. Camion, Ellis Edwards, Hollice Pette-way, James Penn, Luther Tucker, Alphonse Fletcher, Robert Daniel, Theodore Pope, Isiah Dankins.

The Maximus Club, the third social club organized on the campus of the Mobile Training School, was organized for girls of average scholastic ability who possessed no special talents.

The club has now grown into a strong social and literary organization with the purpose of developing in girls the finest qualities of American womanhood. The Maximus Club boasts a roster of 12 members of some of the most talented and cooperative young women in the school.

As their project for the year the club chose to give an album of classical records to the music library.

The music department of the Mobile Training School presented a candle light Christmas carol concert at York Town Baptist Church during the Christmas season. Three choirs were presented. Choir A, directed by Mrs. Yvonne King; Choir B, directed by Mr. George Fletcher; and the Freshman Girls' Glee

Club under the supervision of Mrs. Yvonne King and Mrs. Jeanetta Gaines.

The choir has made two other public appearances this year. The first appearance was for the Interracial Conference at the Ashland Place Methodist Church and the second for the Omega Psi Phi Fraternity's celebration of Negro Achievement Week at Warren Street Methodist Church.

A rich program of vocal music is being cultivated this year. The choirs will do works by such well-known composers as Handel, Mozart, Schubert, Malotte, Wagner and a lengthy repertoire of Negro Spirituals.

The band of the Mobile Training School is making rapid progress under the direction of Mr. Robert Rice, who had them so well trained for the Turkey Day Classic.

Since it is an obvious fact that some students will not complete their high school education adequate provisions are made for those who drop out. By the time a student has had at least a year of mathematics, he is then equipped with the necessary information and skills which will enable him to cope with most practical situations. Too the higher branches are integrated and correlated to the extent that much useful knowledge is gained.

With these things in mind the mathematics department looks forward to a successful academic year.

The Mathematics Department consists of Miss L. M. Davis, R. C. Gaillard and Nathaniel Russell.

ACTIVITIES OF THE ELEMENTARY DEPARTMENT FOR THE FIRST QUARTER

The department raised its quoto in the annual drive with Wilmer Bryant of the 7th Class getting a prize for the Elementary student raising the highest amount.

The sixth class with Mrs. Wise as advisor was given a mammoth party, and she was given a prize for their share in the drive.

The department has been enthusiastic over its Junior Red Cross activities. One-hundred veteran bags have been filled and turned in for the Veterans at Tuskegee.

The following projects have not been unnoticed by the department and an active part has been taken in them. They are as follows:

1. Olk Folk Home.
2. Community Chest.
3. Junior Red Cross enrollment.
4. The Varsity Football Games.

Too much cannot be said of the midget football games played and spirit shown by the department which ended with a "Tony Bowl Classic" held on M. T. S. gridiron.

The team ending the season victoriously with the following record, and declared as co-champions for the season.

Games played 5; Games won, 3; Games tied, 1; Games lost, 1.

Look for the department's second quarter's Honor Roll.

MOBILE TRAINING SCHOOL REPRESENTED AT DISTRICT I. N. H. A. MEETING

Mrs. Addie M. Taylor advisor of Home Economics at the Mobile Training School, Rosetta Everett, president of District II, and Mary White were representatives from the Mobile Training School chapter of the New Homemakers of America.

District I of the State H. H. A. held its first meeting in the auditorium of the State Teachers College, at Montgomery, Alabama. The theme of the meeting was the "National Project," which is the infantile paralysis unit at Tuskegee, Alabama. It was discussed by Mrs. Bettye S. Turner.

This meeting is the third of a series of meetings of the N. H. A. attended by Mrs. Taylor and Miss Everett. The first at Tuskegee and the next which was the national meeting at Langston, Oklahoma.

OUR CAFETERIA

Mobile Training School provides a program for the development of the *whole* child. The account here is evidence of the rich and varied program which plays an important role to that end.

Relatively recently the School Cafeteria has come to be regarded as an integral part of educational experiences. It is the most immediate media through which the concept of proper diet may be developed in a practical way.

In this aspect of the program of the School the Mobile Training School has probably taken the lead of all schools in the system. It seemed that self-help was the only source of improvement at hand. Accordingly, shortly after the opening of school this year, acting upon a faculty committee report who surveyed the cafeteria prior to the opening of school, a drive was launched to provide facilities for serving the students who come here.

As the results of this effort a Commercial type gas range, a steam table, hot water tank and large three-compartment sink for dish washing were installed. These fixtures replace a coal range which formerly was the only facility in this category, except a small sink, present in the cafeteria. For refrigeration, a large 32 cubic foot electric refrigerator is being installed replacing a 100 pound capacity ice box—this fixture was secured through the assistant superintendent's office for a fraction of its initial cost.

The County Student can now be served in beautiful rose colored plastic service with stainless steel silverware. There are brown plastic trays upon which he places his dishes in order to facilitate service.

That these modern cooking and service facilities are now available is a tribute to the organizational skill and ability of county's new principal, J. T. Gaines, the industry and cooperation of the facult and the cooperation of its student personnel. The faculty committee in charge.

The Student Association of the Mobile Training School was organized the first week in October, after having had a temporary council for the first few weeks of school. Since that time the organization has been in full swing with Marion Baynes serving as president of the student body.

The Senate was organized with Mary D. Johnson, senior, being elected as its chairman. The first meeting was devoted to developing home-room programs for the semester. Much study was given to the Mocotionette (a handbook of the schools' program) to introduce to the new students and re-emphasize to the old ones the program of the school. This was found to be interesting as well as beneficial.

MOBILE BEACON-ALABAMA CITIZEN

STUDENTS OF THE MOBILE ASSOCIATION FOR RETARDED CHILDREN--are pictured (in part) in this picture. They are given speical training and attention to make them beneficial to themselves and society in a special way. See full story as dictated to the Beacon by the Principal, Mrs. Grace D. Steinback. (Beacon's staff photo by E. Madison Cockrell)

PART SIX

ORAL HISTORIES

THE UNFORGETTABLE CLARENCE MATTHEWS

Wednesday, April 29, 1970   MOBILE PRESS—1-D

Mobile Press Register Photo By George Edwards

ENTURY OF LIVING — 104-year-old William Lee, who
ves with his daughter, Mrs. John Scott at 500 Osage St.,
ts in the dining room of their home and reminisces
bout memorable experiences of his long lifetime.

MOBILE NEGROES
Discusses Modern Marvels

Moon Too High To Reach,
Says Skeptic Centenarian

By SYLVIA HART
Press Staff Reporter

"I hear tell they've been to the moon, but I still don't
elieve it. It's too high," laughs 104-year-old William Lee of 500
sage St.

The centenarian readily discusses other modern marvels
hich he considers fact, however. A native of Dallas County,
la., he was in his 80s when he saw television for the first time
Mobile.

"Television is all right. It tells you things you never hear
lk of," says the great-grandfather who lives with his daugh-
r, Mrs. John Scott.

airplane. He and his brother-in-law were at a mill making cane
syrup in Ackerville in Wilcox County when the plane flew
overhead.

One of 12 children in his family, Lee says he never had a
chance to go to school much. "Papa made us all work hard,"
he explains.

Later he and his wife "had a crowd of children (12, in
fact); so I still had to work hard," he continues.

The slight built man talks fondly of his wife who, he says,
has been dead "a long time." He explains, "She was a good,
loving woman. We never did quarrel. Both of us was church
people."

A farmer in Ackerville for many years, Lee says when he
went home from the fields at night, his wife always had supper
waiting.

FAMILY SINGING

Usually after the meal, the family plus a school teacher
who boarded with them, sat around the fireplace and talked
and sang.

"I used to sing pretty, but I can't sing now," says Lee. He
relates that various members of the family sometimes played
the guitar during the song sessions. "I couldn't play it though,"
he chuckles.

Besides farming, during his lifetime Lee has laid brick,
painted houses, dug ditches, worked at a sawmill and worked
on the railroad.

"I railroaded for 14 years and never lost a day," he boasts.
He was never sick during that time.

This good health continues even today. The elderly man
complains of cramps in his hands. Otherwise, he has no ail-
ments, he says.

"I just ask God to strengthen me. I ask him from my
heart, and he hears me. God don't pick and choose," he says
with certainty.

Lee, whose father lived to be 109 years old, may have
inherited the tendency toward longevity. But he does not
express this view in answer to the inevitable question, "Why
have you lived so long?"

"I get plenty of rest and exercise, and I worked hard all
my life," is his answer.

MOBILE PRESS 1972

Sought Treasures Over Six Decades

His Game Is Antiques

By SAM MORRIS
Press Staff Reporter

St. Joseph Owens is not as active as a few years ago, but he is still regarded in the trade as an astute dealer in antiques.

Now 76, Owens doesn't take to the streets as in previous years. For more than six decades he was a familiar figure to Mobilians as he rode the city streets aboard his horse and wagon in search of old bargains.

And he found them, too.

The crafty trader made a nice living in antique dealings. He turned a nice profit through the years of buying and selling merchandise, jewelry and goods Mobilians had thought worthless.

His formula, which he revealed during an interview at the home of a daughter, was simple:

"Check for deaths. You could always find bargains at homes where there had just been a funeral."

Some of those everyday bargains, he recalled, would quickly turn in a fine profit. "Once I sold an antique, which I bought for practically nothing, for $800."

"That's the name of the game," quipped Owens as he drifted back to memories of bygone years when he and his late wife, made a profitable business of hard bargaining.

"My wife was the backbone and brains of our partnership,"

See Page 8, Col. 3

ANTIQUE COLLECTION — An 80-year-old African weapon made of teak wood, a 50-year-old butter churn, an African head carving, paintings and tables are just a part of the large antique collection of 76-year-old St. Joseph Owens (above) in Mobile. (Mobile Press Staff Photo by Ron Wheeler)

Latest in Series of Honors

reprint 5/21/70

Mobile Student Named Presidential Scholar

Delphine R. Smith has another honor to add to her growing list.

Yesterday she was named a 1970 Presidential Scholar by President Nixon.

As a special added honor she was invited to the White House June 4.

"Surprised and excited," was the Bishop Toolen High School student's reaction to the announcement. "My parents were also very excited and t h r i l l e d," she commented.

Miss Smith is a recipient of a National Achievement Scholarship from the National Merit Foundation and received a $1,000 scholarship from the Sears - Roebuck Foundation.

In addition she was offered scholarships to Washington University in St. Louis, Mo., L o y o l a University, Xavier University and Newcomb College, all in New Orleans.

DELPHINE SMITH

WHITE HOUSE INVITATION

In a letter to Miss Smith, President Nixon said: " . . . It is a well-earned distinction and I invite you to meet with me at the White House June 4."

A letter to the principal of Toolen noted that Delphine is among 119 students named Presidential Scholars, "representative of the outstanding 1970 secondary school graduates."

Miss Smith has been a Project Opportunity student since the seventh grade. This program helps prepare students for a higher education.

Miss Smith completes her final exams at Toolen tomorrow. Graduation is set May 29.

This fall she plans to enter Newcomb College and study pre-medicine. She is a member of the National Honor Society, is summa cum laude, Nationwide Latin Examination and is president of the Science Club at Toolen.

Miss Smith resides at 303 S. Dearborn St.

Selection of Presidential Scholars was set up in 1964 and students are selected on the basis of scholarship. One boy and girl is selected from each state and from the possessions of the U.S., along with 15 students at large.

*A chauffeur with almost
no education, he taught a
band of poor black youths to
tackle the impossible and make
miracles for themselves*

Unforgettable Clarence Mathews

By Broadus N. Butler

As SOUNDS of the spring festival faded, we boys gathered around a tall, slender man in the schoolyard. He was dressed in Army surplus khakis as were most of us, though some wore secondhand Boy Scout uniforms, the official insignia removed because we were "colored" and this was Mobile, Alabama, 1929.

The good times we had enjoyed this day could not mask the sad fact that as a fund-raiser our festival had been a failure. "Boys," Clarence Mathews began in a soft, firm voice, "I don't believe we'll be able to make our trip to Washington, D.C., this year. But I pledge to you that we will make it next year—and some-

BROADUS N. BUTLER, former head of Dillard University in New Orleans, is today president of the Robert Russa Moton Memorial Institute in Washington, D.C.—a foundation named for the second president of Tuskegee Institute. He knew Clarence Mathews as few other men could.

day soon you'll be Boy Scouts, too."

Looking back, I realize just how improbable were Mr. Mathews' dreams. He was a chauffeur who never went past the fourth grade. Our parents were poor. What money they made barely put food on the table. Yet we believed him.

Mr. Mathews never allowed us to think about the handicaps of poverty and race. "My boys are as good as any in this town," he often said. And we believed that. We found great meaning in the parables he liked to spin. "Take my old Model A Ford," he would say. "It don't look like much alongside the limousines I drive for rich folks. But when the roads are muddy and those big cars get stuck, I get that Model A and we pull 'em out every time."

Mr. Mathews was in his mid-30s when he formed our chapter of the Allen Life Guard, a religious organization for black youths. He made clear from the beginning that his goal was gaining a Boy Scout charter. And he saw the trip to Washington as an achievement so extraordinary that Scout leaders could not deny us a charter. At our meetings we studied the Boy Scout handbook. We formed a bugle corps and drill team, and spent many nights camping in the abandoned brickyard where a young pitcher named Satchel Paige had played his first ball. A good deed a day was mandatory, and Mr. Mathews questioned us closely to ensure that our deeds were for real.

He constantly came up with new challenges. One evening he arranged a debate between me and Kermit McAllister on what type of government best provides for its citizens. My opponent's mastery of the subject left me spellbound. I discovered later that Mr. Mathews had deliberately matched me against a prodigy several years ahead of me in school. It was this kind of challenge that he felt would drive us to achievements higher than we thought possible. He did not want us to be satisfied with anything less than our best.

The trip to Washington was conceived in that vein. He found that, by renting a rail coach, 43 boys could go for $15 each, round trip. For months we worked at odd jobs, saving every nickel and dime we earned. Mr. Mathews had been assured of community support, and he assigned me to collect from a prominent black businessman. This man kept me waiting outside his office for three hours and then handed me a dime. The fund-raising festival was our last hope, but that too failed.

Mr. Mathews did not blame those who had let us down. "Boys," he told us when we gathered to plan anew, "we'll do this ourselves."

The leading daily newspaper in Mobile agreed to pay us 15 cents for every new subscription we obtained. We also distributed flyers for a life-insurance company. My parents, like many other parents, had come to understand just how important this trip could be. Although their combined income was only $20 a month, they were determined to pay for my trip. Every Friday night for weeks they gave fish fries. Profits were low, for there wasn't much money around in those Depression days, but we did manage to raise the $15.

I was lucky. Other boys simply could not produce their share. Even so, Mr. Mathews somehow came up with enough money to take us all on the trip. Late one August night in 1930, 43 of us boarded a rail coach bound for the nation's capital.

The next morning, the train left our coach at a small station outside Chehaw, Ala. "Today we will visit Tuskegee Institute," Mr. Mathews announced, "and you may get to see George Washington Carver." We marched the five miles or so from the station to the college. None of us had ever seen the institute. And we had not imagined that there existed a hospital staffed by black doctors and nurses like the veterans facility at Tuskegee. Visiting Dr. Carver in his laboratory was the greatest thrill of all. We could not hide the pride we felt being in his presence. We marched back to the station singing "Happy Days Are Here Again," for they truly were.

The next day we arrived in Washington, D.C. Night had fallen, and the illuminated dome of the Capitol shone brightly as we stood outside Union Station. The awe filling our hearts, however, was soon replaced with uncertainty. Taxis in the nation's capital did not carry Negroes. For two hours we waited anxiously while Mr. Mathews placed numerous phone calls.

We need not have worried, because this man could surmount any barrier. He contacted the lone black Congressman—Oscar DePriest of Chicago—who personally led the pool of cars that took us to a local church, where we bedded down.

The city did not seem able to imagine how this band of Negro boys had managed to get there from Alabama in the midst of the Depression, and we were welcomed with open arms—and kitchens. Tours were arranged. We climbed the Washington Monument. At the foot of Abraham Lincoln's statue Mr. Mathews led us in prayer.

I was the least accomplished of our buglers but, typically, Mr. Mathews selected me to blow taps at a ceremony we conducted at the Tomb of the Unknown Soldier. "I'm counting on you," he said. And for the first and only time in my life I hit every note.

On our last day in Washington, Mr. Mathews announced that we were going to visit the President of the United States. Unbelievable! But as we were escorted through the front door of the White House, we knew it was true. President Herbert Hoover and Vice President Charles Curtis shook our hands and spoke with each one of us.

Mr. Mathews had opened a whole new world before us. From the halls of Tuskegee to President Hoover's extended hand, we sensed a land of opportunity for those willing to tackle the impossible and make miracles for themselves. It was a lesson that we would never forget.

Word got around in Mobile about all that had happened, and quite a crowd gathered to meet us on our return. And soon the second part of Mr. Mathews' pledge was fulfilled. We were awarded not one Boy Scout charter but three. Mr. Mathews even arranged for us to use the Mobile Scout camping grounds, previously reserved for whites.

These breakthroughs, however, could not surpass the experience of our journey to Washington and the wonder of how Mr. Mathews had accomplished such an impossible dream. Three years later, a small legal notice in a local paper explained how he had done it. A bank was foreclosing a mortgage on his home—a mortgage he had taken out to finance our trip. Several of our parents tried to persuade Mr. Mathews to let them help, but he refused, realizing that they could ill afford to give even token donations. I overheard him tell my father, "This is part of teaching my boys what it means to be a man."

Somehow he managed to keep his home, though he did lose his Model A for a time. But not one of his boys ever lost the meaning of the standards he set for us. In fact, every boy who made that trip to Washington became a success and, in the years before his death in 1958, Mr. Mathews could list many a distinguished career in business, law, education and community service achieved by those whose lives he had touched.

THE FACE OF MOBILE has changed since I lived there. A new convention center stands on the site of the church where our troop met. The brickyard where we camped is now a public-housing project.

But if you visit the playgrounds near that housing project, you'll see a man doing the job Clarence Mathews once performed. In the evening he's out with his boys—often as many as 70 of them. Three years ago he took $400 out of his savings to buy them some football uniforms. Now they are working for a trip to Florida. "I told my boys, 'You're not going to stand out on a street corner and beg for money for this trip. You're going to earn it, and that way it will have meaning for you.' " His name is John, and he's the image of Clarence Mathews—his father.

Plane Song

As OUR PLANE began its descent near Madrid, moisture formed in the cabin and began to fall in steady drops onto the seats. Our eight-year-old daughter sat studying the water inside the plane and the blue sky outside. Then her eyes lighted up, and she turned to us excitedly and said, "That song is right! The rain in Spain *does* fall mainly in the plane."

—Contributed by Miriam Hoff

PART SEVEN

* CHURCHES AND CONGREGATIONS

ENTER TO WORSHIP   Big Zion A.M.E. Zion Church   DEPART TO SERVE

Big Zion Church organization is 111 years old. Has a seating capacity of 1.800

"The Church That Cares"

BIG ZION CHURRAH   1829

— BIG ZION SUNDAY SCHOOL —
1950

131-B-Zion Church SUNDAY School Class (About 1950

BIG ZION CHURCH
CONGREGATION

THE ST. LOUIS STREET BAPTIST CHURCH

This fine church, located on the corner of Dearborn and St. Anthony Streets, the second oldest Baptist church in the city, is pastored by Reverend B. B. Williams

106

…es of members still active who joined the …ring the administration of the fourth colored …v. J. L. Frazier, are Mesdames Martha Sim- …ginia Kittrell, P. A. Butler, Mattie Fore- …Jenkins, Grace Willia…s, Emma Sims, Ma- …Louise Bowman, Rosa Ballard, Lula Davis, …ner, Mary L.   Horace Mc- …ohn Mingo, Coleman Sloane, Leslie Busby, …s, R. H. Perry, Frank Marsh, Dave Morris, …tz. Mrs. Julia Allen is the President of the …Band. The Sunday School and Junior Choir …Mrs. Era Gordon.

The church celebrated its 94th anniversary November 30, 1947. Members of this church are filling positions in practically every field of endeavor. Its twenty or more teachers with Bachelor of Science degrees to Master of Arts degrees, are loyal and plan to have the floor of the main sanctuary of the church painted from proceeds contributed at a Teacher's Service Program to be rendered in January, sponsored by County Supervisor, Mrs. Wilber Weeks Burroughs.

Rev. B. B. Williams, present pastor of the St. Louis Baptist Church. During his ten years of pastoring, two martgages were paid, pastorium renovated twice, old debts to members and former pastors paid and edifice improvements to the amount of Over four hundred members have been add-$30,000 (thirty thousand dollars) or more. ed to the church. Rev. Williams came to the St. Louis Baptist Church from the historic 17th Street Baptist Church, Anniston, Alabama built by Dr. J. H. Eason, former President of the Alabama State Baptist Convention.

Two of the leading church in Georgia were pastored by Rev. Williams before coming to Alabama. Rev. Williams is a product of Morehouse College, Atlanta, Georgia. At present he is Associate Editor of the Mobile Advocate, editor of the Colored Church and School News of the Mobile Press, teacher at Cedar Grove Seminary and Vice-Chairman of the Alabama Baptist Minister's

ST. LOUIS STREET CHURCH

ZION CONFERENCE BIG AFFAIR

shots of the Conference held at the State Street A.M.E. Zion Church were taken on the last day of conference. Sunday, November 16. Conference opened officially on Wednesday, November 12, when r Baumhauer and other key personalities extended a very warm welcome to the delegates.

ministers attending the 74th A.M.E.Z. ference which was held at State Street wn above is a group of out-of-town min to eat their dinner in the basement of

Mrs. Josephine, active State Street Church member, and founder and principal of Allen Institute. Mrs. Allen is also organist for the State Street Church choir.

Bishop Gordan prepares to end his sermon on the last day of the Conference. On the other side of the rostrum is Rev. C. C. Coleman, Pastor-host. The State Street Choir prepares to chant.

delegates eating the delicious food pre m by Mobile church folk. An abundance rful flowers made the tables extremely

Bishop B. M. Gordan of the Ninth Episcopal District relaxes a bit in the study of the State Street parsonage. Bishop Gordan has just preached an excellent ser- mon at the eleven o'clock service.

PART EIGHT

---

*DOCUMENTS AND PICTURES OF THE CIVIL RIGHTS MOVEMENTS

*THE NEGRO PROCLAMATION

135

Bishop W. T. Phillips

IS MOBILE A DESIRABLE CITY And CAN WE AS COLORED PEOPLE LIVE HERE WITHOUT BEING OPPRESSED?

One lesson that many of us should learn is how to live and where we can live best. One must admit that living conditions in the lower southland have not come half up to par for colored people. Nevetheless, many of the traditional prejudices and segregated customs have and are being broken down in a way that members of other races have become more attentive to the dynamic progress the affect has upon the cities and states of the south. In the years to come we shall see a different people.

The privilege of members of other races to see members of the Negro race prove himself

to be more than maids, cook and janitors. The people they've only had the privilege of working with, have awakened to the fact that all people are able to meet the best of the Colored Race in this day and time.

As for Mobile, its relationship with the various races may be comparable with other lower southern cities in that some of its segregated laws are not as strong as others. However it has come a long way and yet a long way to go. A mark of impression came about recently when we were able to see Mobile as it is deep seated when the Freedom Train stopped. There could have never been a finer relationship in a northern city as Mobile opened her doors of Welcome to all citizens regardless of color, to march in single line and view the various constitutional rights of all. This speaks well of the city and its leaders. Long live the spirit that is now existing in Mobile.

When you want to know the truth about Mobile read the "Live Wire"

Bishop W. T. Phillips, Publisher

MOBILE IS OUR CITY, TOO!!!

The undersigned are all Negro citizens of the Mobile area. Many of us have been a part of this community for all of our lives. We like our city. It has beauty, culture and racial understanding.

This understanding is an essential part of our daily life. It enables us to improve our standard of living and to better participate in the activities of our community.

We support the President's call for harmony and an end to racial hatred. We want our fellow citizens to know that we detest violence and anarchy.

Mobile is our city, too, and we will do our part to avoid violence in any form.

Mr. Cornelius Huff	Mrs. T. M. Myers	Johnnie West	Glemen Hopkins Sr.	Jacqueline Morris
Mrs. Lula Huff	Mr. T. M. Myers	Herbert Fairley	Emmett Frank Singleton	Florence Morris
Johnny Huff	Mrs. E. M. Boykin	Cecil Gravely	Albert Sithtt	Harold A. Morris
Mary Margaret Huff	Ann Hemmingway	Claud Brown	Major Osburn Sr.	Jacqueline Williams
Mildred Huff	J. H. Andrews	Sylvester Davis	H. Johnson	Mr. & Mrs. John Henry
Catherine Huff	W. C. Fiely	Ike Fleming	Wilma Marie Simpson	Andry
				Alberta Williams

Keivan Huff
Michael Huff
David Johnson
Gus Laller
F. Warren
Willie Baker
Edward S. Mitchell
W. C. Paul
E. T. Morris
Archie Buckly
Robert Musgrove
George E. Crawford
John M. Sheffield
C. Russell
Jerrie Parfis
Clifton Snowden
Mr. & Mrs. G. C. McRae
Johnny Orso
Joe. Orso
Clifton Morgan
Mrs. Edna Bellamy
Mary M. Thompson
Naomi Taylor
Rosetta Davis
E. Masen
Howard Gaskins
Sdy M. Wells
Jamo Matthews, Jr.
K. Coleman
W. L. Creel
Eloise Creel
Vivian C. Ware
Pratt
Paul Kirkland
Lillian E. White
Alice Hazzard
Johnnie Jackson
Clifton Reid
Julius Robinson
T. Myer
W. Dearmon

Stanfield
M. G. Scott
A. S. Davis
J. E. Ethered, Jr.
M. E. Lewis
H. Mabrey
Viola Williams
Willie Armstead, Jr.
Alphonne Lewis
Fred Perkins
Leonard Milton
Joe B. Martin
Phillip Agee
Joseph Davis, Jr.
Brenda J. Davis
Mellie L Davis
Eddie Davis, Jr.
Jefferson G. Young
Benjamin Roberts
Henry Junior
Caesar Agee
Mrs. Martha Taylor
Mrs. Mitchell Ann Davis
Mr. Solomon Shepard, Jr.
Edward James
Leroy Smif
Irene Gamble
Magell Young
Paul Gray
M. Yeager
Mrs. Inez King
Howard McCaskill
Mrs. Fleater Compton
Mr. Carter Compton
Mr. Man Smith
Mr. Frank James
Mrs. Mary Wish
A. E. Callier
Johnnie S. Wright

Joe Bell Sr.
Louis Count
John D. Chapman
Eugene Rivers
Jossie Rivers
Israel Scott
Roy Bennett
Larry Rennedy
Frank Campbell
James McQueen
Cleste McQueen
James Walter
Annie Walter
Joe Melvin King
Verla Faye Brown
Georgia L King
Harold Brown
Jane Paull
Arthur Poellnits
Willie Poellnits
Fholie Rembert
Camiller Pettway
Pierce Pettway
Marie George
Thomas McDougle
Hosea Waymon
Chester Grice
Ronald Gradford
Janie Huff
Mr. Clarence Carson
Mrs. Hattie Carson
Dianne Robinson
Thomas Brooks
Sylvester Turner
Willie J. Grandisen
J. L Andrews
Albert B. Bunn
Maovette E. Burroughs
Leroy A. Alexander
Ernest Guinn

Zad Douglas
Dot Easley
James Watts
C. F. Caffey
Elizabeth Rascoe
Gladys Bjert
Helen Lane
Robert Watson
F. T. Morgan
Rev. A. W. Erwins
L. B. Ward
Mr. & Mrs. John McKinley
Mr. James Blackmon
Les Whitlock Jr.
R. L Grant
Willie Bright
Floyd Gandy
Nathan C. Simmons
Evelyn Hallan
Cealia M. Jones
Leon Hallomon
James Brown
Lennel Gaillard
Albert McClain
Dudley Hudson
Vonnie Kay Gaillard
Levell Easterling
Lucy Little
Joseph A. La Porte
R. C. Scarbrough
Farris Guest
Luirne Price
Francie Waters
Marilyn Maniel
S. P. Packer
Willie E. Arnold
Ellis Dixon
Rosie Morris
Nathaniel Morris Sr.

Davise Mae Sanders
Rosie Pickens
Frazier Hill
Oliver Gydunc
Blanchard Portis
Howard Coleman
J. B. White
Samuel Austin
Woodrow Austin
Neal Johnson
B. B. Miller
Edna M. Jackson
Bertha Wimsherlg
Gladys Marie Woods
Jennie Mae Elley
David W. Key
Marvin McDowell
Aron Scott
Carolyn Brown
Elizabeth Scott
Jacob East
Ann Davis
Ruby Davis
Love Wright
Vinnie Croswell
Clarence Carter
Juanita Liddell
Mr. Roosevelt Griffin
Mrs. Roosevelt Griffin
Ledger Diamond
William Howard Woker
John D. Scott
Bennie Martin Jr.
Samuel T. Coleman
Jessee Washington
A. Coumpton
C. R. Faircloth
Betty Joyce Glenn
Sheila Jean Williams
Edgar Robinson
James Robinson

The Negro envisages 1945 with a hope that there will be more pronounced examples of inter-racial good-will, fairness and justice than 1944 and other previous years afforded.

Americans of both races must be rational in facing the so-called and overworked "race problem," and should pledge a courageous and incessant campaign against racial and religious intolerance which some people have found conveniently fitted their subtle purposes to exploit certain segments of the nation's population.

We cannot be sincere in professing a firm belief in democracy unless we are willing to practice it at home. The race problem had its beginning in the desire to exploit, and racial antagonism has flourished throughout the years on the assumption that one race has some sort of an inherent right to keep the other down by methods which clearly circumvent the intent and purposes of the laws and Constitution of the United States.

The restlessness of the Southern Negro because of the injustices suffered denying him equal job opportunities, educational privileges, justice in the courts, political rights, and equitable and adequate public facilities and accommodations, cannot be truthfully attributed to "encouragement" from so-called " Northern meddlers." The fact is that there has been a decided improvement in the course of thinking of the Southern Negro and he has begun to feel that the same federal and state governments which have the power to impose the responsibilities regardless of race, color, or creed, of citizenship upon all Americans, can and should likewise extend the common privileges of citizenship to all Americans, irrespective of race, color, or creed.

Negroes in the armed forces are fighting and dying in defense of American ideals just as are others. At home colored citizens are willingly making every contribution to the war effort that white citizens are making. They are also meeting all tax and other obligations levied by the several states, although some of the states have long followed a policy of taxation without representation toward people of color who reside within their borders.

Properly qualified Negroes even now are denied the right to register as and and are not voters, to vote, permitted to exercise rights of citizenship to which they are lawfully entitled. As a whole they are usually victims of miscarriages of justice in the courts, and subjected to other abuses either openly or through subterfuges , merely because of so-called "race."

In view of the deplorable conditions which affect the Negro's status as a citizen, and the apparent reluctance of the powers-that-be to take proper steps to afford prompt relief to the situation, We, the colored citizens of Mobile, assembled on this first day of January 1945, to celebrate the 82nd anniversary of the signing of the Emancipation Proclamation by the immortal President Lincoln, feel that we are compelled to lend our support to nation-wide efforts now being conducted to have the Congress enact legislation to afford all Americans, regardless race, with equal job opportunities, to abolish the poll tax, to make lynching a federal crime, and to provide federal aid to education.

In addition, We feel constrained to decide upon the application of legal redress in instances when and where the Negro has been deprived of the right to register as a voter, or denied the right to cast a ballot, when he can meet equally with others the provisions of the law governing these privileges.

We urge that equal educational opportunities for Negro children and equal salaries for Negro teachers be made available in the State of Alabama and Mobile County.

We further ask that police brutality be curbed by the heads of the law enforcement agencies, and that our courts be temples of justice for all men, regardless of race, color, or creed.

We also urge that equal job opportunities be provided , and that employer and labor union alike be cited before a properly designated agency in instances of against discrimination involving the right to work.

We believe that an expansion of Negro business through cooperative and profit-making enterprises for the purpose of building a security against economic maladjustments, and to help relieve the impending post war problem of unemployment which shall confront the Negro group as well as others, during and after the reconversion period, is essential .

We recommend that local and federal housing authorities provide adequate housing for the Negro people of Mobile, who have been sadly neglected in this particular.

Negroes are urged to buy war bonds for patriotic and thrift reasons, and to render all other assistance possible toward a successful prosecution of the war effort.

We believe that there should be an impartial enforcement of the city ordinance on the seating of the races on buses, and that both white and colored citizens should follow the Golden Rule of justice and fair play on the buses and streets, and in public places, in daily contact.

We insist that Negroes conduct themselves properly in public places and on the buses, or at their places of employment, to give assurance to others that we are entitled to the equal privileges of citizenship which we seek.

We view with apprehension the high homicide rate of Negroes in Mobile County and throughout the South, and look with misgiving upon the usual leniency in sentences in murder cases involving only members of the colored group. We urge that effective steps without brutality be taken to stop the carrying of switch-blade knives, razors, pistols and ice picks, or other dangerous weapons, by those whose public conduct would justify suspicion of being trouble-makers, or who frequent taverns and other public places of ill-repute.

Respectfully submitted,

Citizens Committee of the

National Association for the Advancement

of Colored People, Mobile Branch.

Sponsors of the Eighty-second Anniversary

Celebration of the Emancipation Proclamation

A. S. Crishon, President

W. L. Bolden, Treasurer

J. L. LeFlore, Executive Secretary

Unanimously approved by the approximately 1,000 persons present at the meeting, held at the Aimwell Baptist Church, Monday afternoon, January 1, 1945.

1967

HUEY P. NEWTON
BLACK PANTHER ACTIVIST

MOBILE NEGROES 1970

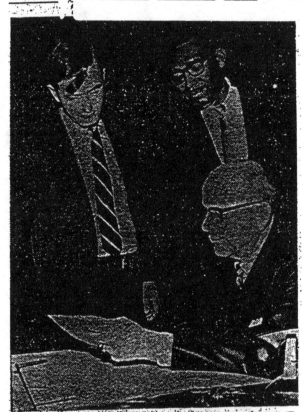

Mobile Press Register Photo By John T. Waits III

NEW DEPUTY MARSHALS — U.S. Marshal H. Stanley Fountain (seated) announced appointment of two new deputy U.S. marshals—Franck A. Shelby, 26, (left) and Frank E. Daffin, 33, both native Mobilians. Daffin, a nine-year veteran of the Mobile Department, is the first member of his race to serve as a deputy U.S. marshal in Mobile since Reconstruction Days, court officials said. Shelby, a veteran of Vietnam service won the Bronze Star for outstanding service as a member of a Military Police company.

1,000 PARTICIPATE AS—

MOBILE HOLDS CIVIL RIGHTS FIRST MARCH

WE SHALL OVERCOME.. is the general mood of these marchers as they sang and chnt in front of Mobile's city Hall on Wednesday May 15th. Their morale is very high and they have high respect and admiration for their unyielding leader. Their voices were heard. THEY WERE NOT GASSED AS PROMISED BY THE POLICE CHIEF. (Photo by Cockrell)

[See story on Page 2]

2,000 STAGE POOR PEOPLES MARCH

Cloudy weather, rain or shine, could not stop the 2,000 marchers of Mobile Saturday at 12:30 p.m. as they marched in support of the Poor People of Mobile and for justice.

Both black and white citizens alike, sang and marched for 3 hours demonstrating to the public the need for jobs and justice in Mobile for its poor. The march was legal and the local law enforcement officers, escorted the marchers in the long trek through black and white neighborhood. The march was also in support of the poor peoples march to Washington D. C.

The march started on Davis Avenue at Hickory Street, and proceeded down Broad Street to Dauphin Street, paused for brief prayer and song service at Dauphin Way Baptist Church, then proceeded to Lafayette, and again to Davis Avenue where a rally was held at the Davis Ave. Recreation Center.

Speakers at the rally were Dr. D. L. Chastang, McKinnon of Mobile County, Baptist, and Rev. J. L. Phillips, pastor of Mt. Sinai Baptist Church, Rev. Chastang gave a powerful and dynamic speech to the crowd while standing in the yard of the Recreation Center.

The powerful praise stressed the importance of the march and the need for more marches if they have to be held every day in the week, until the demands of the poor are met. He stated that a change must be made, a change from acts to words.

MOBILE 10¢ BEACON 10¢
ALABAMA AND CITIZEN
27TH YEAR 47TH EDITION   MOBILE-TUSCALOOSA, SATURDAY, JUNE 1, 1968

POOR PEOPLE'S MARCH HELD HERE—A very successful march was held here last Saturday as an estimated 2,000 black and white persons were in line at some point. This is a view of the front of the parade. At the extreme right is Rev. John Thompson, pastor of the Church of the ... march director and organizer. (Photo by Watts)

By E. Madison Cockrell

Considering himself lucky to be still alive with only minor injuries is Elmore Carter of 4177 Chin Street in Plateau.

Mr. Carter told the BEACON that he was about to leave a Gulf Service Station located at the intersection of Bay Bridge and Telegraph Road and another driver waiting in traffic told him it was safe for him to cross over and get into the lane of traffic in the direction that he was going.

He reiterated that he pulled out and upon pulling out far enough into the street, he saw a car moving the transfer truck coming down the lane that he was crossing, and saw that there was a collision coming that was inevitable, he swerved his auto in a direction to minimize the certain impact and the transfer truck ran into the driver side of the car completely demolishing the left side of the car where he was sitting and tearing the front of the top up from its mounting, completely shattering the plate glass windshield, knocking the right door completely open, slinging the other passenger on the right side of the car out on the ground on her knees (a Miss Rose Kidd), Miss Kidd, who a friend of the Carters, complained of back pain and knee injuries. This accident happened between 9 and 10 o'clock Friday May 24th and they were rushed to hospital by Patricia ...

CONTINUED ON PAGE 2

144

MARCH PASSES DAUPHIN WAY BAPTIST--The Poor People's March last Saturday is shown passing the Dauphin Way Baptist Church where it paused briefly for prayer. There was no disorder and no arrests.   (Photo by Watts)

MARCHERS INCREASE--The ranks of the Poor People's March increased as the parade made its way through the city streets. Many whites joined the ranks to swell its numbers.
         (Photo by Watts)

PART NINE

*NEGROES APPOINTED TO HIGH POSITIONS

obile Press   SECTION B

LOCAL NEWS

RY 1, 1976   — MOBILE PRESS   1976   —PHONE 433-1551

FIRST BLACK APPOINTED — Mobile County Sheriff Tom Purvis, right, announced Wednesday that John McCorvey, 36, would be the new assistant chief deputy in charge of the county jail and the first black appointed to his staff. McCorvey officially takes office New Year's Day. A native Mobilian, McCorvey comes to the Port City from East St. Louis, Ill., where he was a patrolman for the past six years. Purvis denied that McCorvey's being black was the principal reason for the appointment, but did say it was one of the factors in making the selection. (Mobile Press Register Photo by Ron Wheeler)

First Black given chief deputy post

City Appoints Negro Teacher To HR Post

MOBILE PRESS   1970

John F. Gray, social studies teacher in the Mobile public school system for 22 years, was appointed today to the Mobile Housing Board to replace retiring member John L. LeFlore, effective Sept. 1.

GRAY

Gray's term is for a five-year period and there is no salary with the position.

Gray's appointment was announced by Mayor Joe A. Bailey who expressed confidence that Gray will act in the best interest of all the people of Mobile.

Both LeFlore, who has served since 1966, and Gray are Negroes. LeFlore was the first Negro in Mobile to be named to a major policy-making board.

Gray said he intends to do the fair thing for all citizens and work diligently for the progress of the city. He said he feels "the plain, ordinary person has a role in making America great."

MOBILIANS MAKE GOOD — Shown with Loren Green, center, star of TV's "Bonanza" series, are two Mobile brothers who have made a business success in Los Angeles. They are William Newman, left, president of New-Cal Technology, Inc., a black-owned electronics manufacturing firm founded in 1968, and Levon Williams, who is associated with the business. New-Cal will be the first tenant in a new building complex owned by Willowbrook Industrial Properties. Green is one of the general owners of Willowbrook.

Former Mobilians Own New Electronics Firm

Two Mobilians followed the late Horace Greeley's advice and went west to find fame and fortune.

They are William and Levon Newman, sons of Mr. and Mrs. Robert Newman of 1610 Polk St.

William Newman, who graduated from Xavier University with a degree in engineering and did graduate work in electronic engineering at UCLA, is now president of New-Cal Technology, Inc., a black-owned and operated electronics manufacturer. His brother, Levon Newman, is associated with him in that business. Both served in the Army where Levon studied engineering. Both are former newspaper carriers for The Mobile Press Register and graduates of Most Pure Heart of Mary High School here.

New-Cal, located in Los Angeles, manufacturers and sells electronic subsystems and modules. William Newman has been involved since 1956 with the development of solid-state transducers, production engineering, and most recently, evaluation of electro-mechanical components.

His company made news in recent weeks when it signed a contract to become the first tenant in a new building complex owned by Willowbrook Industrial Properties.

The general owners of Willowbrook include the stars of TV's Bonanza — Lorne Green, Dan Blocker and Michael Landon.

152

Colored Men In Armed Forces

Seaman 1/c Joseph Graham wrote his family of 10 N. Dearborne St. recently that he is enjoying good health and is still in the Southwest Pacific. Several months of the more than a year he has been in the Navy have been spent in this area. Seaman Graham attended the public schools of Mobile and was in the employ of the U. S. government when called to the service.

Of the two years Seaman 1/c T. G. Patterson has served in the Navy, 14 months have been in overseas duty. Ribbons and medals for good conduct and bravery in combat are being worn with pride by Seaman Patterson. His mother, Mamie Patterson of Brussels St. is happy to have him home for 30 days and will make his stay pleasant. He worked for Addsco and attended Dunbar High School.

Seaman 1/c Evans Spencer who formerly worked for the GM&O Railroad and who joined the Navy nearly two years ago, is well according to his family of 200 Fourth Ct. Orange Grove Homes. He is serving on a hospital ship in the Southwest Pacific and is striving to do his full duty.

Cpl. Joseph Rogers has been ill from time to time since joining the Army and has been stationed in South Carolina since he was not able to go combat duty. He entered the Army three years ago and worked at Brookley Field prior to his call. Cpl. Rogers attended Owens School. His mother of the Fifth Ct. Orange Grove Homes heard from him last week.

B. L. Reddix of Prichard, aunt of Cpl. Edward R. Green entertained him during the three days he spent in Mobile recently. He came here from Hollinger Field Air Base where he has been stationed most of the 32 months he has served in the Army. Cpl. Green attended Dunbar High and worked at Brookley Field.

Colored Men In Armed Forces

Pfc. Lee M. Mickels has been stationed at New Orleans some of the 33 months he has been in the army. He has seen service in the Southwest Pacific for 22 months, and has been in several engagements. While on a 14-day leave Pfc. Mickels is visiting his brother, Joseph Mickels of 507 N. Conception St. He worked at Brookley Field.

Entering the army three years ago, Pfc. Hubert F. Gwinn has been stationed at several points and is here from Key Field, Miss., on an 18-day leave. He is expecting an early promotion. Pfc. Gwinn attended Dusable High School in Chicago.

Frances Gavin who has been in the Merchant Marine service about a year has just returned from one of the many trips he has taken, some of which have been in the war zone. His relatives of 657 Delaware St., are giving him a hearty welcome. Gavin is a member of Big Zion A. M. E. Z. Church.

Cpl. G. A. Bragg has been overseas most of the year he has served in the army. When last heard from by his family of 209 First Ct. Orange Grove Homes, he was well. Prior to entering the service he worked at Brookley Field and attended Heart of Mary School. He realizes that he is being counted on to give his best for his country.

MOBILE-PRESS 1970

July 9, 1970

SURPRISE JURY ACTION

Mobile civil rights leaders indicted

BY TED PEARSON
News staff writer

MOBILE — Surprise grand jury action ad come today in what police re convinced is a potentially explosive power struggle mong leaders of a militant ivil rights group in Mobile's lack community.

Temporarily interrupting its xhaustive State Docks investigation, the current ounty grand jury has returnd three secret indictments in he wake of an apparent nvestigation of a recent hootout in which leaders of Neighborhood Organized Workers (NOW) were directly nvolved.

THE INDICTMENTS remain secret until arrests are made, and the office of District Attorney Carl M. Booth indicated that arrests may come today.

Formal first-degree murder charges have already been filed against one suspect in the shootout, which left one Negro man dead, riddled with shotgun blasts fired on a street in a predominantly black area.

Held on that charge is Arenza Thigpen, 25, identified by police as a top-ranking official of NOW.

The NOW president, Noble Beasley, who has had close association with other black civil rights leaders in other parts of the country, has been questioned extensively by police because he was, police said, present at the scene of the murder of James Perine, 35, identified by authorities as a top aide to Beasley.

Police made no charges against Beasley, however.

The grand jury moved swiftly into the case Wednesday morning by summoning and questioning witnesses in connection with the shootout. The secret indictments were returned later in the day, and are being processed through the sheriff's department for execution of arrest writs.

BEASLEY, recognized as the most militant and aggressive of the Mobile civil rights leaders, is a nightclub operator. He reportedly is associated with other business enterprises in black community in addition to his activities as NOW president.

In this latter role, he has spearheaded several marches and demonstrations in support of demands for widespread new benefits for blacks.

At the time, police reported the victim of the shootout, Perine, was standing alongside a car in the Toulminville area when another car occupied by Beasley and Thigpen drove up. An initial shotgun blast wounded Thigpen in the arm, police said. A second blast from another shotgun killed Perine.

Police gave scant details of the incident, but said their inquiries indicated the shootout may have climaxed sharp disagreements stemming from a struggle for power among the NOW leaders.

PART TEN

*ADVERTISEMENT 40'S---70'S

SEASON'S GREETINGS

A MESSAGE TO COLORED MOBILE

WEST END CAB COMPANY — purchased the franchise of Pike Cab Company — The two companies have merged and will operate under the trade name of Pike Taxi Company — The entire building located at 815 Davis Avenue with spacious reception room for its patrons.

Safety First
Careful Drivers

24 Hour Service

Courteous Drivers

"DON'T HIKE, RIDE A PIKE"

PIKE TAXI SERVICE

815 DAVIS AVENUE   DIAL 3-4977   MOBILE, ALABAMA

For Good Food and Pleasant Entertainment

Visit The

STREAMLINE CAFE

"Mobile's Most Popular Rendevous"

607 Congress Street   Mobile, Alabama

Dial 2-9666 for Reservations

1950

1968

— 1948 —

Announcing ..

Dial 6-8243

GULLEY'S HOTEL

The Only Colored Hotel in Greater Mobile

Located on Highway 45   Allenville, Alabama

Owned and Operated by Colored — Mr. W. A. Gully, Owner

FINE ACCOMODATIONS

Exterior of the New Gully Hotel
All Outside Rooms

View of the Hotel's Restaurant where Fine Foods are served
with Courtesy and Efficiency.

HARLEM DUKES SOCIAL CLUB OF PRICHARD, ALABAMA PROGRESSIVE

Reading left to right around the table are Mr. Mack Woods, Mr. Ulysses Stallworth, Mr. Eugene Mounger, Mr. Leonard Parrot (President), Mr. Chester McCann, Mr. Warren Mounger and Mr. Glennon Pickens.

The Harlem Dukes Social Club, whose clubhouse is located at 353 Prichard Street, Prichard Alabama, is one of the most progressive social organizations in this area. This group of fine young men own and operate a spacious club, one of the most popular in this district.

Officers and members of the Harlem Dukes Socail Club are Mr. Leonard Parrot, 65 Avenue F, Prichard, President; Mr. Henry Keith, 222 Pleasant Avenue, Mobile, Vice-President; Mr. Eugene Mounger, 70 College Street, Prichard, Treasurer; Mr. James Pickens, Prichard, Secretary; Mr. Mack Woods, Prichard, Business Manager; Mr. Ulysses Stallworth, 69 Avenue F, Prichard, Chaplain; Mr. Chester McCann, 5th Avenue, Prichard, Bartender.

Members are Mr. Warren Mounger, 70 College Street, Prichard; Mr. Glennon Pickens, 168 Avenue F, Prichard; Mr. Felix M. Vaughn, Jr., 72 Avenue E., Prichard; Mr. Wilmer Henderson, 12 Reynolds Avenue, Prichard; Mr. Goebbie Welch, Reynolds Avenue, Prichard; Mr. Joe Malone, Mobile; Mr. Morris Field, Prichard.

The Harlem Dukes Social Club was first organized in 1935 under the same name. The first president was Mr. William Posey. The present club was established in 1945, and received its charter on December 3, 1946. The bulk of members in the club are veterans. Mr. Parrot, president of the club was a member of the Signal Corps, United States Army and served overseas in New Guinea. He states that the purpose of the club is to help promote a better social life among veterans. The Harlem Dukes will give its first ball in February. The sweetheart of the club is Miss Elizabeth Moore.

Members of the Harlem Dukes Social Club pose in front of the bar. Mr. Chester CcCann does an efficient job as bartender.

Patrons in the club having a wonderful time A painting of dancers on the wall is highly decorative. The club has had many repairs and is quite attractive

LONG'S

SAVE, SHOP LONG'S

MINI-PRICES PUTS MONEY IN YOUR BANK! LONG'S MINI-PRICES ARE RIGHT-LESS THAN DISCOUNT PRICES BECAUSE OF LOWER OVERHEAD. YOU CAN'T BEAT THE FOOD DEAL YOU GET, WHEN YOU SHOP **LONG'S**

MARTHA WHITE CORN MEAL
MIX 5 LB BAG **35¢**

LONG'S DELITE QTS
MAYONNAIISE 39¢

JEWELL 3#
SHORTENING 2 cans **1.00**

COUNTRY MAID
ICE CREAM 2 half gal **1.00**

LIGHT CRUST
FLOUR 25# BAG **1.99**

GRADE A SMALL
EGGS 4 DOZ **1.00**

JIM DANDY
GRITS 5# bag **39¢**

SOUND BEAUTY HALVES
SALMON CAN **35¢**

DEL MONTE
PEACHES 3 CANS **1.00**

Fresh PRODUCE TIME

NO.1
TOMATOES LB **19¢**

HOME GROWN YELLOW
SQUASH
CUCUMBERS OR
STRING
BEANS **10¢** LB

ALABAMA 10# BAG
POTATOES 39¢

RIPE
BANANAS LB **10¢**

SUNNYLAND PURE
LARD 4 LB CTN **35¢**

35¢ AJAX
DETERGENT BOX **25¢**

LITE FLUFF
BISCUITS 6 CANS **45¢**

BEST MEAT BEST PRICE IN TOWN

WHOLE FRESH
FRYERS LB **25¢**

FIRST CUT PORK
CHOPS LB **45¢**

ACME SLICED
BACON 2 LBS **89¢**

FROSTY MORN
PICNICS LB **35¢**

LEAN SALT **MEAT**
3 LBS **1.00**

CENTER PIECES SLAB **BACON**
2 LBS **1.00**

HORMEL LITTLE **SIZZLERS**
12. OZ
2 PKGS **1.00**

REGISTER FOR FREE MONEY
GIVEN AWAY EACH WEEK

LONG'S

LOCATED WHERE
THE BARGAINS ARE

137

ATLANTIC FISH & OYSTER CO.

1414 DAVIS AVE.   MOBILE,   ALA.

SPECIAL PRICES

ICE MILK 3 ½ Gal. **1**⁰⁰	**PURE LARD** 4lbs **39¢**
GRADE A WHOLE **FRYERS** LB **27¢**	**OYSTERS** Pint **89¢**
GRADE A SMALL **EGGS** 4 Doz. **1**⁰⁰	PURE **Sausage** 3lbs **89¢**
STRING **BEANS** LB **10¢**	CAN (FROLIC) ALL FLAVORS **DRINK** 6 for **39¢**
6 Ears YELLOW **CORN 39¢**	ROUND WHITE **Potatoes** 5lbs **29¢**
NECK **BONES** 3lbs **39¢**	

FASHION

PART ELEVEN
*DOWN-THE-BAY------------URBAN RENEWAL

165

Central Texas Street Area

Just four years ago the fourth major phase of Mobile's urban renewal program began in the Central Texas Street area which is defined by Canal Street on the north, Broad on the west, North Carolina street on the south, and by Interstate 10 on the east.

Preliminary studies of this area showed it to be one of Mobile's major residential neighborhoods. Yet, these studies found the area to be suffering from blight and deterioration, particularly in the central core where housing was substandard and overcrowded. Schools in the area were outdated and inadequate to meet modern day needs. There was a shortage of playground facilities and welfare and delinquency statics were high. Streets no longer could cope with traffic demands.

On the positive side of the study, however, condition of existing streets were generally good, several thoroughfares did provide traffic continuity through the area, water and other utilities were adequate, and storm sewage systems (except one major ditch) performed creditably.

Housing on the northern and western fringes of this 326-acre residential area reflected a pride of ownership, and planners were able to formulate a program of both clearance and rehabilitation, rather than one of total demolition.

Today, with blighted and substandard housing mostly cleared, the area has an open, park-like appearance. Many of the existing homes have been retained and restored to their original beauty, and construction of new homes in this quiet, tree-shaded neighborhood is evident at a rapidly developing rate. Approximately 50 acres for schools and playgrounds have been set aside in this area.

Some of the old traffic arteries through this area will continue to be utilized. Canal street is currently being completely rebuilt and widened, and soon Washington Avenue, Texas and Virginia streets will be four-laned. Streets throughout the residential neighborhoods have been redirected for more efficient traffic patterns.

The Central Texas Street Area is rapidly reestablishing itself as one of Mobile's more desireable neighborhoods. To date, there has been over $2,123,000 spent by individual property owners in this area, and more will be spent as land is sold and new private housing is constructed practically all of which will be individual homes.

Dwelling units removed 1923
Families relocated to
  private sales housing 598
Families relocated to
  private rental housing 462
Families relocated to
  public housing 152
Families relocated to
  substandard or
  overcrowded housing 0
Families relocated
  out of town or lost 23

PRESENTATION AVAILABLE

The Mobile Housing Board has produced a slide presentation on urban renewal and public housing and the work its social agencies are doing in the Mobile area. This 18-minute presentation is available to interested groups and civic clubs.

Litter and crowded living conditions prevailed in many of the deteriorated inner core areas of Central Texas Street.

Unpainted "shotgun" houses were a familiar sight.

Old houses beyond repair.

Open drainage ditch bisected area.

At left and below are two of the many new homes built in the Central Texas Street Area. Property for new construction is sold as fast as it is cleared.

NEW HOME — This is an example of the many new homes being built by private developers in the Central Texas Street Urban Renewal area. More than $2 million in private funds has been invested in the area. (Mobile Press Register Staff Photo by Frank Chandler)

OLD AND NEW — The house in the foreground is in harmony with its newer neighbors in Central Texas Street. Many older structures have been renovated as part of the urban renewal project. (Mobile Press Register Staff Photo by Frank Chandler)

Urban Renewal—Weigh Factors

By JANIE NOBLES
Press Register Reporter

Take a drive this afternoon that will make you proud you're a Mobilian — and make you wish you could to more for some of your fellow man.

Go into the area bounded by Canal Street, Broad Street, North Carolina Street and Interstate 10 in the eastern part of town.

You'll find yourself looking at some of the most promising and some of the worst conditions this city has to offer.

You'll be in what's called the Central Texas Street Urban Renewal Area — a section which used to be one of the worst concentrations of hard-core poverty in Mobile.

Some of that poverty is still painfully evident.

Some of it has disappeared, thanks to a lot of taxpayers, a lot of residents who wanted to help themselves, and a lot of hard work by federal and local officials, most notably the Mobile Housing Board.

One local man last week said he's always viewed "urban renewal" as "urban ruination."

If what's happening in Central Texas Street is ruination, this city could use more of it.

Urban renewal means "bulldozers" to many of its opponents, who say the program demolishes existing structures without providing adequate replacement.

According to a slide presentation prepared by the Mobile Housing Board, urban renewal has bulldozed "slums, firetraps, eyesores and hideouts for petty criminals."

YOU DECIDE

Come down to Central Texas Street and decide for yourself.

A group of Mobile officials did just that Wednesday, at the invitation of the Housing Board.

The City Commission, several city employes, area homebuilders and Housing Board personnel climbed aboard a former school bus for a tour of the 223 acre area.

What they saw was a mixed bag. Tumbledown hovels, some occupied but most awaiting demolition by the city, and new brick homes share the same neighborhoods.

What's bad in Central Texas Street is very bad.

Several old wood structures have collapsed and lean dangerously. They pose a threat to children playing in the area and to vagrants who might wander in for shelter or a night's sleep.

Vandals clean out the buildings as they are vacated, hauling away plumbing fixtures and stealing bricks. Several of the rickety buildings are supported by as few as four of the original brick foundation posts. Others rest on the ground with all the foundations hauled away.

Pyracantha bushes and morning glory vines trail over derelict houses.

Urban renewal has resulted in a substantial amount of vacant land at this stage of the Central Texas Street project.

Some of it will be left vacant for an undetermined length of time, said James R. Alexander Jr., executive director of the Housing Board.

He explained that one 30-acre site has been earmarked for two schools and a park, and another large site reserved for low-rise housing for the elderly.

As the bus passed the future school site Wednesday, its passengers saw only a mottled black cat prowling among piles of dirt.

For those who want instant redevelopment, it was not encouraging.

On the good side, a large amount of new private construction is going on in the area.

More than $2 million in pri-

vate money has been spent or committed for home building and renovation in Central Texas Street.

Over-all, a total of $32,297,362 in private funds has been invested in urban renewal development.

Renovation loans at a low three per cent interest rate and renovation grants up to $3,500 are available to low-income families through the Department of Housing and Urban Development.

The Housing Board must approve all plans for construction or renovation in urban renewal areas. It is not permitting developers to replace substandard housing with "crackerboxes."

Shotgun housing also is a thing of the past where the board has authority. With few exceptions, the minimum size lot in Central Texas Street is 7,200 square feet for new construction. The minimum allowable lot for existing housing is 5,000 square feet.

As a result, redeveloped areas of Central Texas Street have uncrowded neighborhoods of comfortable-size homes.

New housing in the project area is in the $17,000 to $45,000 range.

NO SHIFTING

Housing Board statistics disprove contentions that urban renewal simply results in shifting slums from one area to another.

The statistics show that 95 per cent of all families displaced from substandard housing are relocated in standard dwellings.

In its total urban renewal program in Mobile, the Housing Board has relocated 2,174 families. Of the total, 856 have purchased private homes, 557 have rented private dwelling units, and 328 have rented public housing.

Only 28 families have moved into other substandard housing. Twenty-two of the families have been "lost," meaning that they have moved without indicating where they were going. Another 53 families moved out of Mobile.

The Central Texas Street urban renewal project is moving on schedule, and is expected to be complete in May, 1976. The Housing Board reports it is selling lots as quickly as they are cleared and platted.

The next four years should see the end of substandard dwellings in Central Texas Street. More important, it should see 95 per cent of those now living in hovels moved into decent housing.

And that, according to the Housing Board, is what urban renewal is all about.

THE NEW LOOK — Substandard housing is disappearing in the Central Texas Street Urban Renewal Area, and is being replaced with comfortable dwellings. Structurally sound homes are not being demolished, but many have been refurbished and brought up to acceptable housing standards. (Mobile Press Register Staff Photo by Frank Chandler)

CONSIGNED TO THE DUMP — The pile of debris pictured above will be hauled to a landfill as the City of Mobile proceeds with clearing lots in Central Texas Street. In the meantime, nails, broken glass and loose timbers litter the area. (Mobile Press Register Staff Photo by Frank Chandler)

Renewal

TEXAS STREET

Here are the anticipated costs on the Texas Street Project:

Acquisition of property _____ $13,700,000

Gross cost of project _____ $23,500,000

Less sale of land _____ $3,400,000

Net cost of project _____ $20,100,000

Less federal grant _____ $18,500,000

Cost to City of Mobile _____ $6,600,000

In regard to the East Church Street Project, which is almost completed, Housing Board officials point out that "the marked changes in this area today are not only outstanding, but nearly incredible."

It was noted that over-all, nearly $20 million has been invested in that urban renewal area by private enterprise and government agencies.

In regard to low-income public housing, the Mobile Housing Board currently operates 3,366 units of public housing in eight separate locations.

According to a progress report for 1968, the board said, "Financially, the operation of these projects are self-sustaining. Cost of administration and the maintenance are paid through rental receipts. In lieu of taxes, the Housing Board pays 10 per cent of all rental income to the city for fire and police protection and other municipal services. Figures show that over the past three years, more than $50,000 annually was paid to the city and the School Board, bringing to over $2 million paid since 1940."

The newest housing project, built at a cost of $5,800,000, is the 450-unit R. V. Taylor Plaza.

MORE DWELLING UNITS

Today, there are 680 new dwelling units in the planning stage. Jesse Thomas Homes will house 380 families in three to six-bedroom apartments. It will soon go under construction on land already purchased within the Water Street Urban Renewal Area north of Beauregard Street. Cost: About $7 million.

In the Central Texas Street Area, 300 low-income units are to be built for the elderly and the handicapped. Funds have already been earmarked for the housing project.

The five members of the Housing Board are: Max W. Morgan, chairman, John L. LeFlore, vice chairman, Joseph H. Wilson, Jr., Charles Bedsole and Norman E. Cox.

Morgan is an analyst at Alcoa and business manager of Local 320, United Steel Workers of America. LeFlore is a retired postal worker and director of the Non-Partisan Voters League. Cox is vice president of Patterson Hardware Co. Bedsole is president of Car Park, Inc., and Wilson is president of Wilson Electric Co.

The operations of the Housing Board are audited annually by the Audit Section of the Department of Housing and Urban Development. The government's General Accounting Office makes spot audits.

Before

Progress made in urban renewal

By KATHY PENDER
Port City Writer

In 1959 there were about 5,000 units of substandard housing in Mobile—houses with inadequate plumbing and wiring, inexpensively constructed and unpainted, often packed closely together. Today that number has decreased to less than 4,000.

The decline in that number is largely due to the urban renewal, public housing and community development projects of the Mobile Housing Board, with most funds coming from the federal government and the City of Mobile doing most of the work.

According to James Alexander, executive director of the board, the living conditions of many Mobilians have been improved at the same time tax revenues on property have increased.

In the Broad-Beauregard Street Avenue urban renewal area, which was completed in 1968, fire calls have been reduced by 99 per cent and tax revenues have increased over 300 per cent, Alexander said.

The housing board itself pumps additional revenue into the city, the director said, at the rate of over $2.5 million since 1940. In lieu of taxes, the board pays ten per cent of all rentals on it's 4,000 public housing units to the city and county.

Alexander is quick to point out the difference in urban renewal and public housing that he finds often misunderstood.

"Urban renewal does not mean public housing," he says. Urban renewal property is usually owned and developed by an individual, not by the Housing Authority. The board however, does maintain architectural control over it.

And, the director adds, "homes in urban renewal areas are not necessarily homes of low-income families."

To qualify for low-income or public housing, such as the Central Plaza Towers and Josephine Allen Homes, a family must be paying 25 per cent or more of their total income for housing.

Besides the Broad-Beauregard Street Avenue urban renewal area, The East Church Street Area, which includes Spanish Plaza, is also complete. In this area many homes were redone by individual families, who purchased the structures from the housing board.

The latest urban renewal efforts have come in the Water Street and Central Texas Street areas. The downtown traffic loop and a new sewerage system, eliminating pollution in the bay are the major achievements Alexander cites in the this downtown central business district area.

The biggest need here, he says, is for private enterprise to purchase land and build in the area. Currently there are 15 acres for sale in the central business district and three industrially zoned acres for sale.

In the Central Texas Street area, which is currently being developed, there are 40 acres of land for sale, Alexander says. Thirty acres are for residential use, six for public use, and six for buffer business and commercial use.

All the property will probably be purchased within two to three years, Alexander says.

In the urban renewal areas Alexander says, not only are new homes built, but streets are paved and areas are set aside for parks and playgrounds.

For example, in the 326-acre residential area which is privately owned in the Texas Street area, about 50 acres have been set aside for schools and playgrounds.

Service to people does not end with a rehabilitated or new house, says Alexander. Social services are also a part of the housing board's function.

"We often follow-up housing with job training and daycare for working mothers," he says.

Because the housing authority receives a great deal of federal funding—$2,756,000 this year and an expected $4.6 million in 1977—federal regulations can pose a problem for the administrative board.

"Now, local officials have the final say in what projects are undertaken and, all over the country people are

scatter shooting to appease a few people here and there.

But he adds, scatter shooting, which refers to the practice of paving a street here and there rather than doing one entire project, is less a problem here because of the good planning involved in urban renewal community development.

"In the masterplan (which was begun in 1949) use of federal money was limited to certain neighborhoods," Alexander explains.

In fact, he says, most of the success of urban renewal in Mobile is due to good planning. The board, which the director says, is ranked high in competence nationwide, received two national awards in 1969—one for its excellent relocation efforts for families displaced by urban renewal and another for outstanding civic improvement.

Seven areas now designated for improvement in the board's community development program are the Bayview Area, Trinity Gardens, Sandtown, De Tonti Square, West Church Street, Demotropolis Road and the restoration of the old City Hospital, which was recently completed and dedicated as the new headquarters for the Mobile County Department of Pensions and Security.

After

MOBILE REGISTER

Metro/Region

Section B

Tuesday, October 18, 1988

Redevelopment efforts win federal awards

By ROYCE HARRISON
Press Register Reporter

One award, a 1988 Certificate of National Merit, goes to the city's Community Development Program for the Central Texas Street Redevelopment Program.

The other award, a 1988 Certificate of National Recognition, goes to the city for the Water Street Redevelopment Project.

While critics decried the city's plunge into Urban Renewal and still frown on the wholesale destruction of architectural history, the city has been tapped to receive two awards from the federal agency that furnished the money two decades ago to tear down rundown buildings.

Old waterfront warehouses and Mobile's south side — two types of redevelopment — disappeared, leaving a once reminded people of a sleepy, Southern port — disappeared, under the builder's blade years ago.

"It just boils down to hard work over the years," said James R. Alexander, executive director of the Mobile Housing Board.

Both awards are expected to be presented Nov. 7.

People may not realize it, but

Investors have sunk more than $100 million into the Water Street and Central Texas Street redevelopment areas in the past two decades, Alexander said. "That's private money."

"That doesn't include any of the public funds," he said.

Most of the investment shows up as houses, he said. The brick houses lining the Central Texas Street area's streets were privately financed and are a far cry from what used to stand there, he said.

"It was the most crowded area in the city. It had the highest tuberculosis rate. It had the highest crime and

paid the lowest taxes, he said. "It's a tremendary benefit of its activities; noteworthy demonstration of its public entrepreneurial spirit; exceptional physical design; promotion of local independence from federal funding and oversight, new approach to encouraging economic or community development and as a model for other communities to follow.

"This award is being given because this project was rated one of the top 20 applications submitted for the national recognition program in Region IV of HUD, which covers eight

See AWARDS, 4B, Col. 1

Awards

■ Continued From Page 1

eastern states.

"After clearing old buildings of of Central Texas Street's 250 acres, the city upgraded drainage and sidewalks, built a major park and playgrounds, provided land for expanding the Allen Memorial Home and other improvements. Almost all of the houses and apartments that were rebuilt are private, Alexander said. The exception is a small public housing project, he said.

"Some buildings weren't torn down when the city in the early 1960s started implementing a redevelopment plan drafted in the 1960s, he said. About 210 houses eligible for rehabilita-

tion were upgraded in bounded by Interstate Canal, Broad and Sou na streets.

Shanklin said coope forts with private also fielded Mobile cate of recognition to opment along Water S

one of the best neighborhoods in Mobile now."

Carter Shanklin, spokesman for the Department of Housing and Urban Development in Birmingham, Ala., described the city's Community Development Program as an outstanding example of public-private partnership.

"The award is for the cooperative efforts of the city and developers in the Central Texas Street Redevelopment Project area," Shanklin said. "Mobile's Community Development Program was selected for the ex-

PART TWELVE

*PORTRAIT OF HENRY ROBINSON—LOST LAND ARTICLES, AND
COURT DOCUMENTS

172

HENRY ROBINSON   1906
LAND OWNER   MONROE COUNTY
ALABAMA

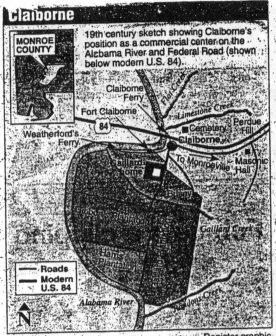

Claiborne

MONROE COUNTY

19th century sketch showing Claiborne's position as a commercial center on the Alabama River and Federal Road (shown below modern U.S. 84).

Claiborne Ferry

Fort Claiborne

Weatherford's Ferry

Limestone Creek

Perdue Hill

Cemetery

Claiborne

To Monroeville

Masonic Hall

Gaillam Creek

Hans Plantation

Alabama River

— Roads
— Modern U.S. 84

N

Register graphic

CONNIE BAGGETT/Press Register

A tombstone of the early 19th century at Claiborne is examined by Kathy McCoy, president of the Monroe County Tourism Board.

ALABAMA HISTORY

Feb 26 96

Reviving Claiborne's wild days

▶ Monroe County board has hopes of turning scene of 19th-century adventure into a tourist stop

By CONNIE BAGGETT
Staff Reporter

CLAIBORNE — High on the east bank of the Alabama River, farmland, timber and residential areas have overtaken much of what this river boom town left behind, but the adventure and intrigue of Claiborne's heyday could soon be a tourist draw for Monroe County.

Today, the site of Claiborne is little more than a marker by U.S. 84 on the bluff overlooking the Alabama River, but, hidden just off the beaten path are remnants of a town that rivaled any metropolitan area in the mid- to early 1800s. The

city missed becoming the state capital by one vote in those days.

Monroe County Tourism Board President Kathy McCoy said the Claiborne site is a long way from drawing crowds, but there is great potential there.

"So many of the families that went on to settle this part of the country passed through here, and some even lived here for a time before traveling on," McCoy said.

"The history here and the river make this an ideal stop along a tour, but there is still a lot of work to be done," she said.

From its early days as Alabama Heights to the scenes of bloody battles in the Creek Indian War to a cotton boom town, Claiborne was a lifeline for the people living for many miles in any direction."

Please see CLAIBORNE on 4A ▶

News tips: 434-8614

Claiborne

▶ Continued from 1A

Settlers from east of the Appalachians passed through the settlement as soon as the Federal Road cut through the wilderness in 1806.

Gen. Ferdinand Claiborne and his troops built the fort that would bear his name in 1813. He came to the area to defend settlers against increasingly violent retaliation by Creek Indians angered about encroachment onto their lands, as historian Henry De Leon Southerland Jr. explains in "The Federal Road."

The fort stood as headquarters for Claiborne and his troops as well as a supply depot. After the Red Sticks were defeated by Claiborne at Holy Ground near Montgomery, the frontier was flooded by settlers eager to carve out a living.

People common to the frontier town were famed Indian fighter Sam Dale, statesman James Dellet, William Barret Travis and others.

Just around the bend from the fort, Sam Dale fought and killed several Red Stick braves with a rifle used as a club.

James Dellet made Claiborne his home before his election to the Alabama Legislature and later to Congress.

He married and began his family here, but lost three of his four children to cholera. His wife died soon after.

His late wife's young cousin served as governess for the Dellet's daughter, and became Dellet's second wife.

Dellet Park, as the house and grounds are known, is currently owned by Mobile attorney Agee S. Broughton III.

An associate and reported student of Dellet's made a name for himself at the Battle of the Alamo in Texas, but not before murder forced him from Claiborne.

William Barret Travis practiced law in Claiborne, but found little happiness in his marriage to Rosanna E. Cato. Marilyn Handley describes her in the Summer/Fall 1995 issue of Legacy (a Monroe County Heritage Museum magazine) as a likely student of Travis at the Claiborne Academy.

Travis was a teacher, lawyer and husband by the age of 21. The next year he became publisher of a newspaper. The publication's success was short-lived, however, as Travis became the focus of a murder trial.

Shortly after Travis' wife became pregnant with their second child, a man believed to be his wife's paramour was murdered. A slave of Dellet's (then the judge) was blamed with the murder, according to local legend and historical accounts.

Travis stepped forward to confess his own guilt before the slave was hanged for the killing. He was allowed by Judge Dellet to leave the state and his young son in 1831. He was 22 years old when he left Alabama. Travis never saw the daughter born after his departure. His wife divorced him a few years later.

The slave, Ben, accompanied Travis to Texas and to the Alamo where Travis perished in battle in 1836.

But scores of well-known citizens and anonymous settlers alike walked the banks of the Alabama at Claiborne.

The town's buildings were constructed largely by slaves. Some slave cabins from the time period still stand today near the sites of plantations.

Claiborne, with a population of 2,500, entertained the Marquis de Lafayette as he toured the frontier in 1825.

By that time, steamboats made regular stops at Claiborne's cotton docks some 180 feet below the bluff. Planters from miles away brought bale after bale of cotton to be shipped to Mobile for sale.

W. Stuart Harris writes in "Dead Towns of Alabama" that Claiborne sported 800 citizens in 1820, more than 2,000 in 1821.

By 1830, the town had two large hotels, a boarding house, jail, many churches and an academy.

Alabama's second Jewish congregation organized at Claiborne and left behind a cemetery after the town's decline following the Civil War.

With King Cotton crushed by Union forces, the trade at Claiborne declined. By 1872, only 350 people remained. Most others, Harris writes, moved to Mobile or elsewhere.

Today, the Masonic Lodge where residents entertained Lafayette still stands. It was moved to Perdue Hill decades ago.

The law office of Travis and another cabin of the time period flank the old lodge.

In Claiborne, the cemeteries are still visible, as is the antebellum home of Dellet.

Most of the site of the town and the fort lie on private property.

Efforts are under way to make the cemeteries — which are public — more accessible, she said, and to open the Masonic Lodge and Travis office for interested visitors.

FEBRUARY 10, 2002

eeting addresses blacks' land losses

em seems to be
g in South, say
tes to Tuskegee
s conference

N BENN
Press

KEGEE, Ala. — Tony Hay,
asn't lost any of his land,
knows black farmers who
nd he shares their con-
er that growing dilemma
outh

problem hit home several
go when he learned of two
sisters who were about to
eir land when a relative in
r state decided to sell his

contacted state forestry
explained the problem
n and then came up with a
buy out the relative and
he sisters to continue liv-
their property

e sisters were involved in
ending partition sale that
have been disastrous for
Although only one piece of
ty was to be sold, the laws
ed that the entire acreage
t intact within the family to
the sale of individual par-
aygood said.

ey thought they'd be
to move, and we were
to develop a strategy to
heir land for them," said
d, who attended Tuske-
niversity's 110th Annual
s Conference on Friday.

t all black farmers are as
te as they were.

eral speakers at the con-
addressed the growing
n of black-owned land loss
the concluding sessions.

Rep. James Clyburn, D-
d, the growing black con-
nal caucus has been acu-
are of the problem and is
g to preserve black-owned

ALVIN BENN/AP, Montgomery Advert

Macon County tree farmer and college president Tony Haygood is concerned about black farmers in the
South losing their land. "Owning this land has given me a sense of appreciation as well as great enjoyment,"
says Haygood, who attended a farmers conference in Tuskegee that addressed the issue last week.

> "We have documented
> 2,000 instances where
> land has been illegally
> and unfairly taken from
> black farmers. Some land
> was taken through
> eminent domain, others
> through partitions."
>
> *U.S. Rep. James Clyburn, D-S.C.*

"We have documented 2,000
instances where land has been illegally and unfairly taken from
black farmers," Clyburn told hun-
dreds of delegates to the conference. "Some land was taken
through eminent domain, others
through partitions."

Saying it was time to light
some candles instead of curs-
ing the darkness, Clyburn indicated that a class action lawsuit
may be filed on behalf of those
black farmers who have lost hun-
dreds of thousands of acres in
past decades.

Clyburn, filling in for U.S. Rep.
Sanford Bishop of Georgia, said
he has had questions about possible reparation payments for
black Americans as a result of
slavery. He said he has no such
reservations when saving black-
owned farmland is involved.

"With reparations the question is who pays, how much is
paid and who gets the money,"
he said. "In the case of black land

loss, we know who got the la
so we know who to sue. What
need now is to find a way to fi
a lawsuit."

Besides using most of his
acres to grow timber, Hayg
also is president of South
Community College in Tuske
a small two-year school. He
he divides his time between
white collar academic job and
blue collar farming operation.

"Owning this land has g
me a sense of appreciatio
well as great enjoyment," he
"My two children can see
benefit of owning their own
one day. They have a real at
ment to it. They love to
through it"

177

Churches sue board for return of land

▶ **Property had been donated for school that is now slated for closing**

Associated Press

PENSACOLA — A group of predominantly black churches is suing for the return of property it donated for a public school that is earmarked for closing. The school is one of only two in Florida to ever qualify as a voucher school.

The First West Florida Baptist District Association this week sued the Escambia County School Board, which has voted to close A.A. Dixon Elementary as a cost-cutting measure.

Dixon is one of two Florida schools, both in Pensacola, that the state declared to be chronically failing in 1999. That allowed about 50 of their students to go to private schools at public expense, but both got off the failing list the next year.

A 1950 deed requires the land to be used for "Negro education."

"If it is no longer used for that purpose, then there's a 'reverter' clause," said the Rev. Frank Jenkins Sr., pastor of Mount Olive Baptist Church, one of 42 Florida Panhandle churches in the association.

But school board attorney Francisco Negron said the deed was written before schools were integrated, so the part of the clause referring to race cannot be enforced.

He has advised school officials that the building must be used only for school purposes, not for storage or administrative offices. No decision has yet been made on how the building will be used.

Some parents and community members are trying to keep Dixon going as a charter school and have asked to use the building.

The school attracted wide attention because of the voucher issue.

Gov. Jeb Bush visited shortly after the program began and former U.S. Attorney General Janet Reno was there Tuesday while campaigning for the Democratic gubernatorial nomination.

Legislature to set up task force on black land loss

By PHILLIP RAWLS
Associated Press Writer

MONTGOMERY — The Alabama Legislature is setting up a task force to study whether the state illegally took land from black residents during the days of when segregation ruled in the South.

A resolution setting up the task force was signed into law Tuesday by Gov. Don Siegelman.

Siegelman's press secretary, Carrie Kurlander, said he supports airing all sides of the land dispute and determining the facts. "When facts are presented to the governor and he determines there is an injustice in any way, he believes a wrong should be set right," she said.

The resolution was introduced by Rep. Thomas Jackson, D-Thomasville, who said he became concerned following a series of stories last year by The Associated Press documenting black land losses across the South.

The resolution passed the House on a voice vote Jan. 17 and won Senate approval on a voice vote Thursday.

"We hope this task force will determine what has actually been taken from people and how to rem-

edy it. If the state has taken land from people, we will ask the state to return the land. The governor can do that with a land patent," Jackson said.

One of the AP stories was about Willie Williams of Sweet Water.

The Williams family lost a pair of 40-acre plots to the state in a 1964 court case. The state had claimed the property didn't belong to the family because of a 1906 federal designation as swampland.

Today, the land is vacant, overgrown and posted with signs of state ownership. Some of the area has been opened to timber cutters, state records show.

The AP reported that the family held an 1874 deed and had records dating from the 1950s to show they had been paying taxes on the land for generations. A judge called the state's claim a "severe injustice," but the land went to the state.

Jackson said he has talked to Williams and many other present and former Alabama residents who believe their land may have been taken illegally or immorally.

Sen. Hank Sanders, D-Selma, guided the resolution through the Senate. Sanders, an attorney, said he had worked on some land disputes and believes thousands of people could be affected by the

task force's work.

Jackson hopes to have the 10-member African-American Land Loss Task Force organized by July. It is supposed to report its findings to the Legislature in March 2003. The committee does not have the power to return any land.

One member of the task force would be appointed by the governor, three by legislative leaders, three by the Legislative Black Caucus and one each by the presidents of three historically black universities: Alabama State University, Alabama A&M University and Tuskegee University.

— MOBILE REGISTER 4/2002

IN THE CIRCUIT COURT OF MONROE COUNTY, ALABAMA

MARJORIE JONES, EMRICH KENNY,*
ALFREDA CRAWFORD, and
HENRY PORTIS   *

     Plaintiffs,   *

Vs.   *   Civil Action No.

                                                 *

                                                 *

     Defendants.

COMPLAINT FOR SALE FOR DIVISION

1.   This action is brought pursuant to Sections 35-6-20 to 35-6-25 of the Code of Alabama, 1975 and the Plaintiffs invoke the equity jurisdiction of the Court for this purpose.

2.   The parties are tenants in common of the following described property situated in the Town of Claiborne, Monroe County, Alabama:

All of lots Number 14 and 15 in said Town, according to the map thereof lying West of the public road from Alabama River leading to Perdue Hill, and that part of the Lot Numbered 13 adjoining Lot number 14 and lying west of said road, being bounded on the north by the fence separating the lands of N. C. Thames from the place now known as the Dawson Place (which place is hereby conveyed), being the southwest quarter of said Lot number 13, all of Lot 8 lying southeast of Torrey Branch; all of Lots 9 and 10 lying south of Torrey Spring Branch; also about fifteen acres in the easterly part of the southeast quarter of Section 36, Township 7, Range 5 East, being bounded on the south by the private wood road known as the Torrey Wood Road, crossing the Torrey Bridge Branch in the easterly part of said Southeast quarter of Section 36 and on the east by the line separating said Section 36 from Section 31, Township 7, Range 6 East; on the north by lands formerly conveyed by E. L. Smith to J. G. Sewell; also that a regular tract of land lying in the Northwest quarter and Southwest quarter of Section 31, Township 7, Range 6 East, containing twenty-two acres more or less, bounded on the South by lands now or formerly owned by one King Cole and on the north by a portion of the South boundary line of the Town of Claiborne. Also ten acres of land in the west part of the Southwest quarter of Section 31, Township 7, Range 6 East, bounded on the west by the north line dividing Section 36, Township 7, Range 5 from Section 31, Township 7, Range 6 East; and on the South by Torrey Wood Road leading from the Forks of the Stockton and Monroeville Roads to the Torrey Bridge just west of the said north and south line all of said lands containing about eighty acres, and being land formerly owned by the children and heirs of the late R. C. Torrey. Also twenty acre, more or less, bounded on the east by premises formerly owned by R. I. Draughon, on the south by premises of the late J. M. Lindsey; on the west by premises lately of R. C. Torrey and L. Gibbons; being the land deed by L. Gibbons July 28th, 1875. And five acres described as follows: Bounded on the east by the township line dividing section 36, Township 7, Range 5 from Section 31, Township 7, Range 6; on the north by the Torrey Wood Road; on the west by the Torrey Bridge Branch; on the south by aforesaid land; above lands being described by the surveyor as follows: (Ten acres in the west side of the southeast quarter of Section 31, Township 7, Range 6;) nine acres in the east side of the east half of the southeast quarter of Section 36, Township 7, Range 5; five acres in the east side of the east half of Southeast quarter of Section 36, Township7, range 5; being the same land conveyed to C. P. Dawson by A. Shiff and wife by deed dated March 17, 1899; and the same lands conveyed to the said F. J. Powell by Mary A. Hybart and Samuel C. Hybart, her husband, by deed dated the month of December, 1905.

3.   The parties respective interests in said property are believed by the

Plaintiffs herein to be as follows:

Marjorie Jones   3/64
Emrich Kenny   3/64
Alfreda Crawford   1/64
Henry Portis   1/64

4.   The subject matter property, because of its character, variety of

uses, diverse fractional ownership, and other factors is incapable of being

equitably divided or partitioned between the parties.

5.   The Plaintiffs have employed Noel J. Nelson, Attorney at Law, as

Plaintiffs' attorney, to file this complaint and to prosecute this action for a sale of the said property for a division of the proceeds among the parties, for the mutual benefit of all parties. Further, that said attorney is entitled to a reasonable fee for his services in this proceeding, and that such fee should be paid out of the proceeds of the sale of said property.

WHEREFORE, the Plaintiff prays that the Court will order as follows:

(i)   That the Court will order a sale of said property; and

(ii)   That the Court will order a division of the net sales proceeds of such sale among the parties according to their respective interests after payment and discharge of any valid liens, costs of this action and any Court ordered expenses such as survey and appraisal fees; and

(iii)   That the Court will award Plaintiffs' attorney a reasonable fee for his services in this action to be paid out of the sale proceeds; and

(iv)   That the Court will enter such other orders, judgments and decrees as may be just and proper, the premises considered.

NOEL J. NELSON
Attorney at Law
Post Office Box 2573
Mobile, AL 36652
(334) 433-7272

Please Serve the Defendants by Certified Mail as follows:

A. ...
...
Post Office Box ...
Perdue Hill, Alabama 36470

STATE OF ALABAMA
COUNTY OF MOBILE

Before me, the undersigned notary public, personally appeared EMRICH KENNY, who is known to me and who, after being duly sworn, did depose and say under oath as follows:

My name is Emrich Kenny and I am the same Emrich Kenny named as Plaintiff in the foregoing styled complaint against, A. R. and Nancy Boroughs, Defendants, that I have read and signed the foregoing Complaint and that the matters and facts contained therein are true and correct to the best of my knowledge, information and belief.

_____
Emrich Kenny

Sworn to and subscribed before me this 4th day of February, 2002.

_____
Notary Public

This book was written to provide a narrative and illustrative view of a Culture and History of Blacks during the 40's, 50's 60's and 70's in Mobile, Alabama. There are highlights of how life in an area called Down-The-Bay including an in depth view of how land was stolen from Blacks in the South during this period.

This narrative and illustrative view is based on personal experiences, historical documents, and oral histories. Other sources for the book ``WHO ARE YOU, STAKING A CLAIM IN THIS LAND?'' are as follows: Mrs. Jewel Lawson who assisted with organization, The Mobile Press Archive, The Mobile Register Archive, The Monroe County Courthouse, The Clark County Courthouse, The Mobile Public Library, The Mobile Beacon Archive, The Mobile On Review Archive, Readers' Digest Archive, and the archives from Dunbar, Central, Heart Of Mary and Mobile County Training High Schools.

It is the authors desire to instill pride and knowledge of how life was in the South and in particular Mobile, Alabama. It is also hoped that it will encourage others to solve questionable land deals that may have occurred during that time period.

REFERENCES

Akbar, NA'IM (1984). <u>Chains And Images Of Psychological Slavery</u>. New Jersey: New Mind Productions.

Barker, Lucius. (1991). <u>African Americans And The American Political System 4th Edition</u>. New Jersey: Prentice Hall.

Black, Helen. (2000). <u>Old Souls: Aged Women, Proverty And Experiences Of God.</u> New York: Aldine DeGruyter.

Countryman, Edward. (1999). <u>How Did Some American Slavery Begin?</u> Boston: Bedman: St. Martin.

Finberbine, Roy. (1997). <u>Sources Of The African American Past.</u> New York: Longman

Franklin, John H. (1993). <u>The Color Cone: Legacy For The Twenty-First Century</u>: London: University of Missouri; Press.

Gregory, Dick. (2000). <u>Callus: A Memoir Of My Soul.</u> Atlanta, Georgia: Long Street Press.

Hook, Bell. (1993). <u>A Woman Mourning Song.</u> New York: Harlem River Press.

Horton, Paulette D. (1991) <u>The Davis Avenue Story. The Place, the People, The Memories.</u> Mobile, Alabama: Horton Publishing.

Hurmence, Belinda. (1984). <u>My Folks Don't Want Me To Talk About Slavery</u>. Winston Salem, North Carolina: John H. Blair Publisher.

Jet Book: <u>This Week In Black History. Christopher Handy:</u> May 19, 2003: pg. 20

Kunjufu, Jawana. (1996). <u>Restoring The Village, Values And Commitment: Solution For The Black Family.</u> New York: Longman.

Kunjufu, Jawana. (1998). <u>Sankofa: Stories Of Power, Hope And Joy.</u> Chicago: African American Images.

Peters, James S. (1994). <u>Meaning Of A Black Southern New Englander.</u> Pennsylvania: Dorrance Publishing Company.

Staples, Robert. (1994). <u>The Black Family: Essays And Studies 5th Edition.</u> California: Wansworth Publishing Company.

184

WHO ARE YOU, STAKING A CLAIM IN THIS LAND?

THIS BOOK IS A JOURNEY OF BLACK EXPERIENCES IN A SECLUDED AREA CALLED DOWN-THE-BAY IN MOBILE, ALABAMA. AT ITS' CONCLUSION, HOPEFULLY READERS WILL BE ABLE TO RELATE AND POSSIBLY DEPICT SIMILARITIES TO THEIR NEIGHBORHOOD EXPERIENCES. IN TIMES LIKE THESE, IF OUR STORIES ARE NOT TOLD THEY WILL BE LOST FOREVER, SO WE MUST TAKE TIME TO PUT PEN TO HAND. OUR CHILDREN MUST UNDERSTAND OUR STRUGGLES AND THAT OUR NEIGHBORHOODS WERE ONCE ONE LARGE FAMILY. IT WAS A LARGE FAMILY HELD TOGETHER BY TRADITION, LOVE, PRIDE, AND A STRONG CONNECTION WITH THE SPIRIT OF GOD. WHAT HAS HAPPEN TO US? WHAT HAS CAUSED US TO LOSE OUR WAY? WE MUST TELL OUR STORY, NOT TO RELIVE THE PAST BUT TO STAND STRONG UPON THE SHOULDERS OF THE PAST. THIS IS NEEDED SO OUR CHILDREN WILL HAVE A BRIGHT FUTURE WHERE GOD, HISTORY, FAMILY, EDUCATION, ECONOMIC STABILITY AND LAND OWNERSHIP ARE IMPORTANT.

MARJORIE KENNY JONES IS A RETIRED SCHOOL TEACHER WITH 32 YEARS OF TEACHING EXPERIENCE IN THE BALDWIN AND MARENGO COUNTY SCHOOL SYSTEM. SHE IS A FORMER CONSULTANT FOR THE HEADSTART. SHE EARNED A BACHELOR OF SCIENCE AND MASTER OF EDUCATION DEGREE FROM ALABAMA STATE UNIVERSITY, MONTGOMERY, ALABAMA. A FORMER DOWN-THE-BAY RESIDENT—560 SOUTH WARREN STREET.

DENISE DAVENPORTE MCADORY HAS WORKED 32 YEARS IN THE MENTAL HEALTH FIELD; A CONSULTANT FOR THE PUBLIC SCHOOL SYSTEM, AND A FORMER CONSULTANT FOR HEADSTART. SHE EARNED A B.A. DEGREE IN PSYCHOLOGY FROM KNOXVILLE COLLEGE, KNOXVILLE, TENNESSEE; M.A. DEGREE IN COUNSELING FROM THE UNIVERSITY OF SOUTH ALABAMA, MOBILE, ALABAMA; M.A. DEGREE IN MARRIAGE AND FAMILY COUNSELING FROM MOBILE COLLEGE, MOBILE, ALABAMA AND A PH.D. DEGREE IN FAMILY PSYCHOSOCIAL GERONTOLOGY FROM THE UNION INSTITUTE, CINCINNATTI, OHIO. A FORMER DOWN-THE-BAY RESIDENT—806 DELAWARE STREET.

THIS BOOK WILL:
* TAP INTO OUR LOST CULTURE
* COMPLIMENT SIMILAR EXPERIENCES
* CHALLENGE YOU TO CONSULT WITH FAMILY ELDERS
* STRESS THE IMPORTANCE OF FAMILY
* ENCOURAGE CHURCH INVOLVEMENT
* LOOK INTO LOST LAND DEALS

185

Printed in the United States
By Bookmasters